Child Care
in the Family

**Carnegie Council
on Children Publications**

Published by Academic Press

Child Care in the Family: A Review of Research and Some Propositions for Policy by Alison Clarke-Stewart (Fall, 1977)

Minority Education and Caste: The American System in Cross-Cultural Perspective by John U. Ogbu (Winter, 1978)

Handicapped Children in America (tentative title) by John Gliedman and William Roth (Fall, 1978)

Published by Harcourt Brace Jovanovich*

All Our Children: The American Family Under Pressure by Kenneth Keniston and the Carnegie Council on Children (Fall, 1977)

Small Futures: Inequality, Children and the Failure of Liberal Reform by Richard H. de Lone and the Carnegie Council on Children (Spring, 1978)

Growing Up American by Joan Costello, Phyllis LaFarge, and the Carnegie Council on Children (Fall, 1978)

*Harcourt Brace Jovanovich, Publishers
757 Third Avenue, New York, New York 10017

Child Care in the Family

A REVIEW OF RESEARCH AND SOME PROPOSITIONS FOR POLICY

Alison Clarke-Stewart
Department of Education
University of Chicago
Chicago, Illinois

ACADEMIC PRESS   New York   San Francisco   London   1977

A Subsidiary of Harcourt Brace Jovanovich, Publishers

The writing of this book was made possible by
funds granted by Carnegie Corporation of New York
for the Carnegie Council on Children. The
statements made and views expressed are solely
the responsibility of the author.

✓

ACADEMIC PRESS, INC.
111 Fifth Avenue, New York, New York 10003

United Kingdom Edition published by
ACADEMIC PRESS, INC. (LONDON) LTD.
24/28 Oval Road, London NW1

Library of Congress Cataloging in Publication Data

Clarke-Stewart, Alison,   Date
      Child care in the family.

      Bibliography: p.
      Includes index.
      1.   Child development.   2.   Children—Management.
3.   Children in the United States.   4.   Children—Care
and hygiene.   I.   Title.
HQ792.U5C56   649'.1   77-12797
ISBN 0—12—175250—X

Carnegie Council on Children

The Carnegie Council on Children was established in 1972 by the educational foundation known as Carnegie Corporation of New York to undertake a five-year investigation of what American society is doing to and for children, and what government, business, and individuals can do to protect and support family life. An independent study group, the Council is headed by Kenneth Keniston, the psychologist noted for his studies of dissenting youth and social change, and consists of individuals whose professional interests range from education and medicine to law and economics. *Child Care in the Family* is one of several works done under the Council's sponsorship.

Members of the Carnegie Council on Children

Contents

Foreword

When the Carnegie Council on Children began its work in 1972, a thorough review of what had been learned about children in families was a high priority. In the last decades there has been vast growth in research on child development, and, rightly or wrongly, such research has been used to support proposals for policy affecting children and families. Accordingly, a critical review of the research on family influence on children's development and of the implications of the research for policy was undertaken.

Dr. Clarke-Stewart's work makes clear the strengths and limitations of existing knowledge. As she points out, a vast amount has now been learned about how parents influence children and vice versa. Her sure-handed summary of this research and her criticism of its limitations and biases provide a starting point and agenda for investigators in this field. So, also, her careful drawing out of the policy implications of this research will provide guidance for those concerned with policy affecting children.

But equally important are the limitations of this research. These limitations are of two types: first, potentially remediable flaws and biases in the research itself; second, inherent difficulties in moving from research findings to more normative policy goals and programs.

Of all the problems of research noted by Dr. Clarke-Stewart, the lack of awareness of the context of child development stands out as the most glaring. Parent–child relations are undeniably important, but the setting in which they occur may be the crucial factor determining their effect. "Setting" and "context" mean at least two things. First, no isolated type of behavior on the part of caregivers has any invariant effect on children: the consequences of any single kind of action depend on what *else* is happening between parents and children and on what they bring to their interaction. Words such as "permissiveness" and "strictness" point to caregiver behavior whose impact on children depends on the rest of the parent–child relationship: its warmth or distance, the involvement or indifference of the caregivers, the temperament of the child. The earlier search for simple cause-and-effect relationships (e.g., breast-feeding produces optimistic children) has increasingly been abandoned for studies of the whole caregiver–child relationship in which each type of caregiver–child interaction is studied in the context of all other interaction patterns.

The second meaning of "context" has so far been less studied. This is the "ecological" context within which an entire caregiver–child relationship takes place. The "ecology" of families is exceedingly complex. It includes everything from the quality of family housing to the job (or lack of job) of the parent; from the organization of the neighborhood to the parents' race; from the parents' sense of economic security (or insecurity) to their pride (or discomfort) in their heritage.

These extrafamilial factors and forces affect children in two ways. In part, they directly determine the caregivers' behavior. (For example, a discouraged father who cannot find a job can hardly be expected to be an ebullient, responsive, optimistic parent.) And, in part, they indirectly determine the meaning a child assigns to any given pattern of caregivers' behavior. As John Ogbu points out in another study done for the Carnegie Council on Children,* parental support for outstanding school performance has different effects in black and in white families. Black children face a caste-based system of job ceilings and promotion barriers that has limited the adult payoff of black school achievement; no such ceilings and barriers lie ahead for white children because of their race. It is this broader context of socioeconomic discrimination that crucially determines the consequences of parental encouragement of school achievement.

In principle, research can study the effects of intrafamily context and of extrafamilial ecology on child development, although, as Dr. Clarke-Stewart notes, such research is notoriously difficult, time-consuming, and expensive. Less easy to solve, even in principle, is the problem of drawing policy conclusions from even the best, most contextual research. The core of the problem is simple: there is no

*Ogbu, John U. *Minority Education and Caste: The American System in Cross-Cultural Perspective.* New York: Academic Press, 1978.

logical way to draw conclusions about what *should be* from a knowledge of what *is*. Policy and programs involve questions of *should*—
normative and value issues—while research at best tells us only about
what *is*. Thus, drawing policy conclusions from research findings
necessarily involves the added step of invoking values about the
kinds of people and the kind of society we cherish. No amount of
research can choose or define these values for us.

Sometimes our agreement on values in this country is beyond
question. We commonly agree, for example, that physical health and
vitality is a value—a "right"—for all children. Given this agreement,
research is indeed helpful in defining the antecedents of reduced
vitality, in pinpointing poverty-related factors such as malnutrition,
inadequate prenatal care, low birth weight, and early pregnancy as
factors that tend to lower a child's chances for health and physical
vitality.

But oftentimes our agreement on values is far from unanimous.
Beneath disagreements on the proper role of government in encouraging or discouraging extraparental child care are real value differences about the place of a cooperative, communal orientation as
contrasted to a more competitive, individualistic outlook, with day
care in a group setting alleged to encourage the former. Many de-
bates on public school policy are grounded in value disagreements
on whether (or at what age) children should be encouraged to challenge authoritative ideas, values, and people. Recognizing this, Dr.
Clarke-Stewart sets out her own values and urges that *all* policy
discussions should articulate their goals, including "the kind of children or adults we are creating and the kind we want."

Dr. Clarke-Stewart's work is important for two reasons. First, it
summarizes and integrates in a masterly way what is known about
caregiver–child interactions, drawing from this synthesis a set of
broad implications for policy. But equally important is its critique of
existing research and its understanding of the limits of *any* research
in defining policy. The call for "more research" is a common academic reaction to conflicts in the area of child and family policy. This
book clearly implies that research is only a necessary beginning. In
the end, a better society for children requires not just more knowledge but a commitment to change.

Kenneth Keniston
CHAIRMAN AND DIRECTOR,
CARNEGIE COUNCIL ON CHILDREN

Preface

Concerned people across the nation are asking what social science can tell them about current conditions of childhood in the United States, how adults can help or hinder children's development, what constitutes "good" child care, and what policies of child welfare or early education might effectively enhance children's opportunities for growth. This book is one response to their questions. It brings together the findings of research on the characteristics and behavior of family members that affect children's psychological development (Part 1) and, drawing on that research, offers some comments on child-care policy (Part 2).

The book also addresses the difficulties and dangers of using current research for formulating propositions for policy (Chapters IV and VI). This theme emerged as the task of applying child development research to child-care policy was attempted and it became clear to me that the gap between social science and public policy is indeed broad. The gap in this particular field results largely from the fact that the relevant research was seldom designed to answer policy questions, its goal being to describe the natural course of child development rather than to examine how environments to support, enhance, or facilitate development might be provided—or destroyed—through deliberate intervention or social policy. In trying to apply the data from this body of research to policy issues, it became increasingly apparent that current research in child development is not adequate for the task. As "basic" researchers, it seems, we have been asking the wrong questions, in the wrong ways, of the wrong people—if we hope to help develop public policy.

As of now, the *simple* translation of current research data into policies is impossible. Scientific evidence is artificial, descriptive, and probabilistic; policy is real, causative, and affects individuals. In addition, research in the field of child development has been limited by significant biases: sample selection in basic child development research, for example, has typically been restricted to children in white, middle-class, nuclear families, whereas policies are applied to and affect children in all types of families and circumstances. Unacknowledged middle-class values pervade both research conceptualizations and policy decisions. Today, "science" is popularly invoked as a twentieth-century talisman of truth; its evidence is assumed to be factual, value-free, and infallible. In psychological research, however, the "facts" one expects to derive from science are not yet available. To claim they are gives an illusion of certainty that is misleading and perhaps even dangerous.

This is not to suggest that social science or psychological research is not useful in enlightening policy makers. It can provide valuable perspectives of skepticism and thoughtful inquiry, and add supporting evidence or cautionary notes for proposed policies and programs. It is important to realize, however, that our knowledge of child development and its causes is still tentative, and even more important that application of even the limited knowledge we do possess is problematic. This does not mean that—in the future—research cannot be used as a basis for policy decisions. But if it is to serve that purpose, we will have to make policy questions the direct focus of some research endeavors, broaden research samples to include the kinds of people most likely to be affected by particular policies, enrich our assessment procedures to measure aspects of children's development not covered by eye movement recordings and IQ scores, increase the scope of background factors studied to reflect broader influences on children's lives, and invent or select research designs that will more appropriately evaluate the effects of direct and indirect interventions on children's development.

The message that emerges from this attempt to base policy recommendations on psychological data, therefore, is directed not just to "policy makers" but to "research makers," and, particularly, to students who will be the policy makers and researchers of tomorrow. They should use this book to raise questions and to increase their awareness of problems inherent in the process of applying social science to policy.

This book was written at the request of a group of people who asked me to present the results of research on children's development in the family and to derive some recommendations for policy from those empirical results. To fulfill the request it was necessary to ignore the results of other relevant research and to take at face value the research reviewed, As I have already stated, the data presently available were not ideal for this purpose. Consequently, I did not feel it possible to make specific policy recommendations suitable for implementation; that is not the aim of the policy comments presented in Part 2. What did seem possible was, rather, to formulate a set of policy propositions. As propositions they are open to, need, and deserve careful scrutiny, analytic examination, and extensive testing. They are presented not as "the" policy implications of the material reviewed nor as infallible and factual "scientific rules" for policy. They are *propositions* that were suggested to me by the results of the research I reviewed, and are presented in order to provide ideas and some guidelines for deliberations on policies—in home or state—that might affect the future development of young children in this country.

Alison Clarke-Stewart

Acknowledgments

This book stems from a report prepared for the Carnegie Council on Children, in New Haven, Connecticut, in 1973 and 1974. The opportunity to work with that stimulating group of scholars and humanitarians was an experience for which I am grateful. I am indebted especially to my colleagues and friends Kenneth Keniston, Joan Costello, and William Kessen for their helpful suggestions and support at that time. I am also appreciative of the wisdom later provided by Susan Stodolsky and Joseph Glick who alerted me to certain unintended implications in the original report, and to Ross Parke and William Kessen, again, for suggestions that greatly aided preparation of the final manuscript for the book.

Child Care
in the Family

Part 1

REVIEW OF RESEARCH

I

Introduction

The review that follows is not a comprehensive survey of *all* social science research on child care and development. It is restricted to research examining how children's psychological development is influenced by characteristics and behavior of members of their family. It focuses on "normal" children in "typical" families in America; data from clinical, biographical, and cross-cultural sources are not included. The level of analysis is psychological and behavioral; sociological and economic research is not included. Moreover, since the purpose of the review was to generalize to the broadest possible extent, the details, technicalities, methodological intricacies, and theoretical fine points of individual studies are not emphasized. The empirical generalizations presented are clearly limited by disciplinary bias, cultural relativity, and the need to make consensual simplifications; they represent just one interpretation of a single body of data. Although the body of data is substantial, its limitations should be borne in mind. The review is also generally limited to discussion of the *immediate* effects of families on children's behavior. This is not because of any belief that adult outcomes are not important, but partly out of conviction that they are not *all* that is important, partly because of the inadequacy of retrospective data collection used in most studies that relate adult behavior to child-rearing practices, and partly because the limited data available from longitudinal research do suggest that it is possible—at least for some significant dimensions—to extrapolate from the child at age six or nine to the adult he or she will become.

Four periods of childhood provide an organizational framework for the review of research: infancy (the first six months), early childhood (from about six months to three years), the preschool period (from three to six years), and the early school years (six to nine years). Within each of these age periods the research on children's development in the areas of physical-motor skills, intellectual and language development, and social relations—as they are related to family size, structure, and socioeconomic status and to the behavior and attitudes of parents toward children—is examined. These divisions are all somewhat arbitrary: chronological boundaries are never completely adequate; developments in all areas of psychological functioning are highly interrelated; and within the family all variables interact in complicated ways. Nevertheless, such categorization seemed a useful way of organizing this extremely complex subject.

A brief outline of the recent history of research on early child care provides a background for the review. In the late 1930's, clinical investigators first focused attention on the grim effects of institutionalization. Children living in orphanages and asylums, who were "deprived of a mother's love," were observed to be pale, wan, apathetic, and retarded in physical, mental, and social development. It was soon realized, however, that these children were deprived of much more than a mother's love. Their physical surroundings were perceptually sterile. They had few toys or objects to manipulate. There was some doubt about the adequacy of their diet. They were given little opportunity to develop motor skills. In addition, they were generally lacking responsive or stimulating contact with any adult—not just their mothers. Moreover, they often differed from the home-reared children with whom they were compared in terms of heredity, history, and health. Early investigators did not, or could not, separate these confounding conditions. Consequently, although the studies were socially valuable in drawing attention to the detrimental effects of institutionalization, they were not too helpful in establishing critical dimensions of adequate or optimal caregiving. In the ensuing years, because of the lack of control over these confounding environmental variables and a disregard for factors such as the length of stay in the institution, the constitutional vulnerability or resilience of individual children, and the circumstances precipitating institutionalization, contradictory findings on the effects of institutions appeared. (More recently, researchers have examined children of families of different socioeconomic levels and have tried to draw conclusions on the effects of socioeconomic "deprivation"; such studies suffer from the same difficulties and flaws as the studies of children in institutions.)

Following the period of research on institutionalization, the next approach to the study of early child care to gain popularity was to compare groups of children whose child-rearing experiences had differed on some single, presumably central, dimension. Since psychoanalysis stressed infants' early oral and anal experiences, and learning theory emphasized primary biological drives such as hunger and elimination, logical areas of investigation were feeding practices and toilet training. For at least two reasons these studies did not reveal significant and replicable findings on parent–child relationships. First, gross caretaking practices such as feeding (i.e., schedule of feeding, bottle versus breast feeding, or age of weaning) and toilet training (i.e., early or late) are not unitary dimensions, but are accompanied by and thus complicated by other variations in maternal behavior and attitudes—variations which subsequent research has suggested are more important than the method of caretaking *per se*. Second, analysis merely of differences between groups is a method of limited usefulness for studying complex relationships. At this point, many researchers turned to studying maternal attitudes. Unfortunately, they did not often measure the behavior which translated these attitudes to the child. These attempts, too, therefore, were seldom fruitful in revealing relations between characteristics of caregivers and children.

The next major research approach was inspired by the focus of psychology in the 1950's and 1960's on perceptual-cognitive development. All kinds of easily observed and quantified maternal behaviors which stimulate the infant's senses, such as touching and talking, were measured and related to children's behavior. Much useful information has been derived from such studies, but they, too, are open to criticism on several grounds. One problem with such studies is their tendency to make assertions about parent–child relationships based on examination of very limited numbers of variables rather than after consideration of more complex multivariate patterns of parental behavior or child development.

The most recent trend in research on child care is to study more closely the *quality* of stimulation provided by the parents or the environment. This effort has been directed at analyzing effects of affective and responsive parental behavior. There has also been a growing awareness of the *interactive* nature of parent–child relations. We have finally broken away from the assumption that the world molds and shapes the formless infant, and are beginning to examine the contribution made by the infant to interaction and development. Since most data on parent-child relations are correlational, it is usually difficult to separate cause from effect. But there are increasingly frequent attempts to do so by studying innate individual differences among newborns, by analyzing temporal changes in parent-child relations, and by deliberately controlling and manipulating specific parental behaviors.

It is from the perspective of these most recent research trends and developments that this review attempts to synthesize data from past investigations. That is, an attempt has been made to be *comprehensive,* to search for *repeated* relations, to describe broad *patterns* of relations rather than to list correlations between single pairs of behaviors, and to consider the child and the family as truly *interactive.* Criticism of the methods and research designs of individual studies is not detailed in the report, although it was crucial in compiling the data, as it influenced the relative weight given particular findings. Some general comments on issues of method and design in the study of family–child interaction might be helpful, therefore, for readers who are not familiar with this area of research.

The field is, in fact, one beset by methodological problems—arising at all stages of the research endeavor: design, conception of variables, sampling, recording, compiling, analyzing, and interpreting data. Strategies of data collection which are not based on direct observation (for example, parental interviews and questionnaires and retrospective case studies) are not sensitive to the behavioral dynamics of interaction. They may even be misleading since they often involve selective recall, difficult discriminations and syntheses, and possible distortions on the part of the reporter (usually the mother) or researcher. When direct observation of family interaction is used, there are still problems of lack of standardization (in the home), confounding effects of unfamiliar setting (in the laboratory), and always the possible distorting effects of the presence of an observer. These latter problems—inherent in the very nature of research on family interactions—are unavoidable. Recently strategies have been pro-

posed for minimizing these problems, such as making repeated observations both in natural settings (at home) and in a variety of standardized or semistructured situations (test and laboratory). Distortion
ascribable to the presence of the observer, it has been proposed, may
be minimized by having observers who are similar to the parent (for
example, in sex, race, and age), who are inconspicuous, nonthreatening, friendly, and who visit the family regularly.

The complexity of family-child interaction also creates problems in
selecting variables to study. Some researchers have ignored the problem by assessing gross categories, such as "social class" or "caretaking style," that are themselves complex and inadequately understood. More suitable measures are at the level of observable behavior.
Investigations which are appropriately behavioral in level, however,
have typically avoided complexity by measuring only very simple
variables such as sensory capacities or motor behaviors—easy to observe, but not very interesting or central to children's psychological
development. Yet other investigations have focused on isolated pairs
of single dimensions, such as maternal attentiveness and infant crying or maternal discipline and children's exploration. Since different
kinds of maternal behavior, and children's behavior as well, are often
very highly intercorrelated, no conclusions about specific, critical
parent–child relations can follow from these studies. The best solu-
tion to the problem of variable selection currently seems to be to
examine a wide variety of family variables in a single study, thus
preserving some aspects of the natural complexity of interaction and
providing a context for viewing particular parent–child relationships
of interest. This strategy calls for the use of multivariate statistical
analyses to find behavioral patterns and clusters within the complex
array of measures.

In attempting to reduce complexity, investigators have also sometimes not taken fully into account many relevant variables, such as
family structure, birth order, environmental stimulation, and parents'
education, ethnicity, and religion. Virtually no studies have accounted for *all* relevant variables. Only studies which attempt to
control those variables which are not under investigation can provide
definitive evidence about the variables which are being examined. As
our brief review of the history of research in this area would suggest,
this problem is particularly common in studies which consist of simple comparisons of two populations that differ in some one obvious

dimension (for example, socioeconomic or institutional status), but which fail to consider other ways in which the populations differ (for example, geographical location, health, and race).

More problems arise in choosing methods for measuring the variables selected for study. Many studies have relied on observers' ratings of rather global concepts such as parental "warmth" or "responsiveness." Such a technique is highly subject to observer bias and leads to serious problems of replicability and generalizability. A more satisfactory method of measurement involves operationalization of such concepts and quantification of specific relevant behaviors. Even when behavior is quantified, however, loss of information may occur when a limited selection is made from the behavior stream or when a restricted, preestablished behavioral checklist is used for data collection.

Information is also lost when the continuity of individual development is not preserved through longitudinal investigation. Unfortunately, studies have seldom been longitudinal in design, and when longitudinal, parental behavior has sometimes been measured at one time and infant performance at another. The optimal method of measuring variables in the study of family interaction probably involves continuous recording of concurrent behavior of parent (or sibling) and child, using techniques that preserve the interactive sequences of such behavior. Studies which follow families for a significant length of time rather than just recording interactions during a single observational session provide data on the course of individual development and can be analyzed for causal, dynamic, changing family relations. Longitudinal, observational research can often also be profitably combined with experimental paradigms that focus on some particular critical issue. By deliberately manipulating conditions in the immediate family environment it is possible to assess hypothesized effects on children's behavior. Such experimental studies can thus give support to causal relations suggested by observation of family interaction.

The foregoing methodological problems and proposed solutions were taken into account in compiling the data in this review. Current standards for "good" research were used to filter out dubious evidence and greatest weight was given to data from research which met those stringent criteria. Most weight was thus given to research which was quantitative, empirical, observational, longitudinal, recent, replicated, and comprehensive. Data from questionnaires and interviews were included if they agreed with or enriched observational and experimental data. Although almost any individual study included in the review is subject to some methodological criticism, the attempt made to find consensual evidence from a number of independent investigations would seem to justify some confidence in the empirical generalizations presented. Having lost the nuances and subtle distinctions of individual studies, however, those generalizations are regrettably oversimplified.

II

Research

Infancy: The First Six Months

"Depriving" Environments

Although studies of the *lack* of adequate child care do not by themselves identify the critical dimensions of caregiving, they are useful in establishing the lower limits of child care necessary for normal development. Research on deprivation of care includes investigations of the effects of social isolation, neglect, institutionalization, separation from mother, and perceptual, cultural or socioeconomic deprivation. From the infant's point of view there is not a great deal of difference. Until he or she is able to discriminate social from nonsocial stimulation (after the first few months), it is all perceptual to the baby; and until he or she forms an attachment to one specific caregiver (after six months), it may not much matter who is providing the care. Even under circumstances of deprivation that occur in institutions where infants are seldom spoken to, played with, cuddled, or responded to, and where each is cared for by a number of different people, infants appear to develop normally for about the first three months, so long as their physical needs are met. Only after that age do deficiencies start to appear: motor development is slightly retarded; the infant in the institution does not smile as early as his home-reared peers; speech sounds, especially consonant sounds, after the initial babbling stage, are fewer; and crying is more frequent. In general, immaturity is prolonged. These effects are cumulative and increase with age. They are, however, apparently reversible if the infant is placed in a home or given supplementary caretaker attention and stimulation before he or she is past six months of age. (Ainsworth, 1962, 1973; Aldrich et al., 1945 a, b, 1946; Ambrose, 1961; Bakwin, 1942, 1949; Bakwin & Bakwin, 1960; Bowlby, 1958; Brodbeck & Irwin, 1946; Bronfenbrenner, 1968; Casler, 1961, 1968; Clarke & Clarke, 1960; Dennis & Najarian, 1957; Dennis & Sayegh, 1965; Freud & Burlingham, 1944; Gardner et al., 1961; Gewirtz, 1965; Provence & Lipton, 1962; Rabin, 1964; Rheingold, 1961; Schaffer, 1958; Yarrow, 1961.)

Another dimension of possible deprivation that has received attention from researchers in the past 15 years is that implied by low socioeconomic status (SES). Psychological studies have frequently examined differences in children's and parents' behavior that are related to the father's occupation, income, and education. Such studies typically have contrasted "lower-class" families in which parents have a relatively low level of income and education, and, when employed, work as unskilled labor; "working-class" families in which parents are better educated, more affluent, and the father works in a skilled, blue-collar capacity; and "middle-class" families that have a relatively high level of income and education and in which the father is employed in a white-collar, executive, or professional position. It must be clearly stated in advance that assertions on the effects of social class on child development can be misleading, for at best such statements represent only probabilities not inevitabilities. Moreover, even those probabilities are not very high, as variation within socioeconomic groups is greater than that among groups. Studies of socioeconomic variation are reviewed only because they are useful in indicating the range of family conditions that exist in America, and because, similar to studies of institutionalization, they provide some of the outside pieces of the child-care jigsaw puzzle.

Critics of lower-class families have often assumed that child care in these homes is comparable to that provided in "depriving" institutions. Behavioral differences among infants from different socioeconomic levels have seldom been observed, however; and, in fact, when differences have been noted, they more often favor the infant from the less affluent family—contrary to what one might expect from the child's later performance. There are apparently no significant differences related to socioeconomic status in maternal responsiveness, affection, or amount of talk directed to the infant. In comparative investigations, mothers with less education and income have been observed to touch and hold their infants more, to smile and look at them more often than middle-class mothers. Their infants tend to move and smile more and cry less, and are able to tune out redundant stimulation sooner. Judging from a number of investigations, for infants' normal emotional and cognitive development in the first six months, the environment in most low-income homes is not depriving, and may even be more adequate than in the typical middle-class home. The only differences which may be related subsequently to advanced behavior in middle-class children involve the quality of vocal interchanges between mother and infant. Middle-class mothers are more likely to talk to the infant when they are close together and not doing anything else, and to respond to the infant's vocalizations with speech, whereas mothers from low-income families are more likely to respond with a touch. Infants, moreover, seem to react differently to the mother's talking, although the overall amount of infant vocalization is the same in different socioeconomic groups. When the mother speaks to them, infants from middle-class families are more likely to "listen" (stop vocalizing), whereas infants from families of lower SES are more apt to continue or begin vocalizing.

From this research, the points to be emphasized are that during infancy differences in the behavior of parents and children related to socioeconomic status are relatively small and do not seem to favor infants in middle-class homes. (Brodbeck & Irwin, 1946; Caldwell, 1967; Deutsch, 1973; Golden & Birns, 1968; Hindley, 1970; Kagan, 1968; Levine et al., 1967; Lewis & Freedle, 1972; Lewis & Wilson, 1971; Moss et al., 1969; Seltzer, 1971; Wachs et al., 1971.)

Recently, however, a number of researchers investigating the interplay of biological and environmental factors in human development have pointed to the importance of the interaction of SES with perinatal and postnatal vulnerability (infant mortality, birth weight, birth conditions, and child abuse). High risk babies apparently do better in a low risk—that is, high socioeconomic—environment. Thus, although the typical *behavior* of parents in different socioeconomic groups may not differ significantly at this age, other conditions associated with SES (poverty, father absence, health, nutrition) may have important consequences in infant development. (Bronfenbrenner, 1975; Garbarino, 1976; Sameroff & Chandler, 1975).

Effects of Maternal Behavior

EFFECTS ON PHYSICAL-MOTOR DEVELOPMENT.   In the first year of life the infant changes from a physically weak and relatively helpless creature to one who can manipulate objects, sit and stand, crawl and walk. Our question here is: Are there factors in the mother's behavior which impede or facilitate that development?

In the area of physical-motor development, perhaps more than any other, one is struck by the importance of innate, biological differences among infants. At birth, infants possess different patterns of activity, rhythmicity, sleeping, eating, and eliminating; these basic patterns persist over the first six months. It seems likely, in fact, that these physical characteristics of the infant have more influence on the behavior of caregivers than the reverse. In one study, for example, maternal responses (smiling and talking to the infant), thought at first to derive from maternal attitudes, were judged on further analysis to be accounted for by the infant's physical behavior (in this case sucking). In other studies the newborn's "cuddliness" predicted subsequent maternal behavior. If there is an effect of maternal behavior on physical-motor development it seems to come from giving the infant freedom, opportunities, and incentives to move and to explore. Even when motor development is impeded by physical restriction of movement, however, the result is a temporary retardation that disappears when the child becomes independently mobile. Specific training or supplementary handling and tactile stimulation apparently benefit the infant's motor development only if there is a cognitive component involved (for example, visually directed reaching but not just reaching). For the most part it seems that the infant's motor development progresses through self-rewarding experience in situations which he or she controls, and is enhanced by the provision of opportunities for such experience.

Little information was available in the literature reviewed about children's later motor development, but it seems likely that although specialized motor skills may be enhanced by training and practice, general overall motor development is under biological, maturational control, and if children are given adequate health care and nutrition, physical freedom and locomotor opportunities, their motor development will be normal. (Appleton *et al.*, 1975; Brazelton *et al.*, 1969; Casler, 1965; Dennis, 1938, 1941, 1960; Fogel & Kaye, 1973; Freud & Burlingham, 1944; Geber, 1958; Levy, 1958; McGraw, 1935; Rheingold, 1961; Robertson, 1962; Thomas *et al.*, 1963; White, 1966; Williams & Scott, 1953; Yarrow, 1961.)

EFFECTS ON COGNITIVE DEVELOPMENT. In the area of perceptual-cognitive development, too, it is obvious that innate characteristics of the newborn—such as sensory threshold, perceptual responsiveness, tendency to approach new stimuli, attention span, and persistence—interact with the environment to determine the infant's progress. Unlike motor development, however, cognitive development seems to be significantly shaped by the mother's behavior. Even at this early age, maternal stimulation is highly related to measures of the infant's overall development and IQ (based largely on ability to manipulate simple objects and responses to visual and auditory stimuli) and to measures of specific aspects of the infant's perceptual responsiveness and cognitive development. The more the mother and infant interact actively, though *not* the more time they spend in the same room or in routine caretaking activities, the higher is the infant's IQ score. Cognitive development seems to be related to stimulating maternal behavior, particularly looking at, talking to, and playing with the baby, more than to physical holding and handling, emotional behavior (positive or negative), or the exclusiveness, consistency, or skill of the mother as caregiver.

Quality of stimulation is also important. Measures of the mother's adaptation of stimulation (so that it is appropriate for or "matches" the infant's developmental level and thus his or her ability to comprehend and to respond) are even more closely related to infants' IQ than are measures of the sheer amount of maternal stimulation. Variety of stimulation provided by the mother predicts infants' IQ and exploration of novel objects better than does the complexity and responsiveness of the physical environment or the number of toys available. Finally, the responsiveness of the mother's behavior to the infant's expressive signals like crying or vocalizing, too, is consistently related to measures of cognitive development. In fact, in experimental situations, stimulation that is responsive to the infant's behavior significantly increases exploration, whereas stimulation that is not contingent upon the infants' behavior does not. The suggestion has been made, and fairly well supported, that in order for an infant to be willing to explore new stimuli—which is a prerequisite for further cognitive development and for doing well in test situations—he must learn that his behavior can control the environment, and must come to expect and anticipate control in new situations. This learning occurs through experiencing predictable interaction sequences with the people and objects in the environment.

The relation between stimulation and IQ has been found repeatedly both in studies in which mothers and infants are observed interacting naturally at home and in experimental situations which expose infants to controlled stimulation. Experimentally increasing visual and tactile stimulation has been found to significantly improve the test performance of infants in institutions. How much such increased stimulation would advance the development of infants in adequate homes is not known; it may be that supplementary stimulation beyond the level provided by "good" mothers would be redundant and unnecessary. One point that does seem clear is that at this age the stimulation need not come from the permanent mother-figure. Nurses, research assistants, and principal investigators can all apparently effect changes in infants' performance. When infants are hospitalized they typically show a decrement in IQ scores until they return home; if, however, they are separated from their mothers and placed in a "baby home" where caretakers are attentive and responsive, no decline is observed. Presumably the reason for the decrement in test scores is the infants' lowered motivation to perform rather than any decrease in "ability." This may be the result either of lack of stimulation in the hospital or of the abrupt shift to an unpredictable and unresponsive environment. (Appleton *et al.*, 1975; Caldwell, 1964; Casler, 1965; Chodorkoff, 1960; Dennis & Sayegh, 1965; Geber, 1958; Lewis & Goldberg, 1969; Osofsky & Danzger, 1974; Ottinger *et al.*, 1968; Rheingold, 1963; Rubenstein, 1967; Schaffer, 1965; White, 1966; Yarrow *et al.*, 1971; Yarrow & Goodwin, 1965.)

EFFECTS ON VOCALIZATION.   To some extent, infants' early vocalization is independent of the environment. At the initial cooing and babbling stage, vocalization is not a communicative behavior—even though parents tend to respond to it as such—and most vocalization occurs in nonsocial situations. In the early months babbling seems to be related to the presence of *any* kind of stimulation. It is not surprising, therefore, that for several months the babbling of infants of deaf parents (and even of deaf infants) is not significantly different from that of babies born to parents who can hear. By three months of age, however, infants' vocal behavior reflects their verbal environment. It is not the amount of talking the infant is exposed to that shapes vocalization, but speech directed *at* the infant and *following* his or her babbling. A number of laboratory experiments have been performed to analyze the effects of adult behavior on infants' vocal sounds. They demonstrate clearly that reinforcement increases the frequency of all vocalization and of particular speech sounds as well (glottal stops, "ba-ba," cooing, "umm," and so on). It is necessary, however, that such reinforcement be contingent upon (i.e., consistently follow) the infant's vocalization and be mediated by a person who looks at the infant. The most effective form of reinforcement is verbal, but smiling, touching, and feeding can also increase vocal behavior. Eventually vocalization becomes differentially directed to specific persons; presumably most of the infant's vocalizations are directed to those who have responded most frequently and effectively to previous vocal behavior.

Lest one dismiss as inconsequential the babbling of infants, it should be noted that this behavior, in girls, at least, is related to later verbal proficiency. This fact raises the controversial issue of gender-related capabilities, one of which is language ability. Even at this age female infants, although they vocalize to the same *degree* as boys, are advanced in language *skill,* judging by their ability to discriminate between speech directed to them and that not directed to them. This may be related to the fact that their mothers talk to them more, respond more often to their vocalizations, and are more likely to respond to their behavior with speech. The causal direction of this relationship has not been established. It is plausible, however, that such maternal behavior helps establish the female infants' early sensitivity to language. (Ainsworth, 1973; Bloom & Erickson, 1971; Brazelton *et al.,* 1969; Casler, 1965; Caudill, 1969, Cazden, 1966; Chodorkoff, 1960; Gewirtz & Gewirtz, 1965; Harper, 1971; Haugan & McIntire, 1972; Jones & Moss, 1971; Lenneberg *et al.,* 1965; Lewis, 1972; Lewis & Freedle, 1972; Rheingold, 1961; Rheingold *et al.,* 1959; Ventis, unpublished data; Wahler, 1969; Weisberg, 1963; Wolff, 1963; Yarrow *et al.,* 1971.)

EFFECTS ON SOCIAL DEVELOPMENT. The infant's expressive social behavior—crying, smiling, looking, expressive gesturing—is an exceedingly potent elicitor of immediate parental behavior and has far-reaching consequences for the child's subsequent development. Of all aspects of infant behavior, it most clearly demonstrates the complicated interplay between the newborn's predispositions and the parent's prior attitudes, together forming complex reciprocal behavior patterns which interact and change over time. It is in the area of social development that we see most clearly the impact of infant on caregiver and thus appreciate most fully the comment "the value of marriage is not that adults produce children, but that children produce adults."

Crying is usually the infant's very first expressive behavior, and from then on it is a demanding stimulus to which nearly all parents respond eventually. The promptness of the response to that signal, however, is critical. Contrary to predictions of folk wisdom or some interpretations of operant conditioning, it has been suggested that the immediate and consistent response of the caretaker to the infant's expressions of distress does not "spoil the child" or reinforce crying behavior; rather, it results in more effective soothing and, over time, fewer crying episodes. Physical contact seems to be the most effective response (unless the infant is hungry), but any kind of human contact (voice or face) is usually soothing. The quality of contact is important; more effective soothing is tender, careful, and not too abrupt, brief, or extreme. Initially, in the first three months, the mother's behavior (at least the lower limits of her behavior) tends to be under the infant's control. The infant cries; the mother responds. Gradually, however, if she has responded consistently and contingently, the mother acquires reinforcement value and is thus increasingly able to regulate the infant's behavior. During the same time period the infant begins to expect the mother to respond and learns that his or her needs will be satisfied through social interaction. Thus early reciprocal interaction with the mother may serve as a basis for relating to other people. Research indicates that infants whose mothers are responsive to their social expressions, as well as crying less frequently, develop other modes of communication (physical and vocal), and respond more maturely under stress.

The infant's smile—as well as his cry—has a magical effect on parents and contributes significantly to their humanizing. A smile both elicits and is elicited by responsive social behavior of adults, and thus it increases the likelihood that parents will come near and interact with the infant. Although the smile is a built-in motor pattern, and smiling often occurs spontaneously in the newborn period, it seems to be elicited later by some stimuli more readily than others—stimuli which are usually provided by family members. At six weeks of age, high voices, nodding faces or masks, and touching or rocking make the infant smile; by the end of the third month, effective eliciting stimuli have become restricted to the human voice and face; and, after that, to the voice and face of particular familiar persons. Besides being elicited by these particular stimuli, the overall frequency of smiling may be increased by contingent reinforcement, particularly by picking up, holding, and rocking the baby when he or she smiles. (In fact, contingent reinforcement of any infant behavior is often accompanied by the infant's smiling—apparently as the infant perceives his control over the environment.) Finally, it has been observed that the frequency of the infant's smiling and laughing is related to the parent's frequent expression of positive emotion, and that smiling typically occurs in an atmosphere charged with a high level of positive affect. It is clear that for most infants the mother is of central importance as an elicitor and reinforcer of smiling and as the creator of a positively affective environment.

The beginning of eye-to-eye contact between mother and infant is a critical social development during the first six months. The age at which the phenomenon first appears and the frequency with which the interchange occurs are determined jointly by the predispositions of mother (indicated by prenatal attitudes) and infant (predicted by innate tendency to gaze or gaze aversion). It is not related to the amount of time spent in caretaking activities—during which mother and infant typically are at a 45 degree orientation to one another—but is related to the time they spend playing together, since this activity is almost invariably face-to-face. Once eye-to-eye contact is established, it has ramifications for both participants. Mothers who have previously spent little time playing with their infants suddenly—within days—begin doing so. The adult now perceives the infant as "human" and becomes dramatically more involved with him or her. The amount of eye-to-eye contact between mother and infant is related not only to the quality of the mother–infant relation in the first six months, but also to the infant's subsequent development of social responsiveness and attachment to the mother in the next six months.

One other line of research that emphasizes the early relation between mother and infant takes as its starting point the effect of early contact with the newborn on the mother's subsequent development. Adults, as well as infants, clearly, develop emotional attachments— one of the strongest being that of a mother for her child. A growing body of literature now suggests that even from the first hours after the infant's birth the amount and kind of interaction between mother and infant affect the subsequent course of their mutual attachment. If mothers are separated from their newborn infants immediately after birth, they tend to spend less time *en face* with their infants when they are together during the first few days. Moreover, even months later, these mothers appear relatively less attached to their infants. What is demonstrated over and over again by the research on infants' social behavior in the first six months is the complex, dynamic, and recip-rocal relation that exists between mother and infant. To restrict dis-cussion to the presumed or predicted "effects" of maternal behavior on infants' social development is clearly inadequate and may be even impossible. (Ainsworth, 1963, 1973; Aldrich *et al.*, 1945 a, b, 1946; R. Bell, 1971; S. Bell, 1971; Bell & Ainsworth, 1972; Bernal, 1972; Brackbill, 1958; Caldwell *et al.*, 1963; Escalona, 1952, 1965; Kennell *et al.*, 1975; Leifer *et al.*, 1972; Moss, 1967; Moss & Robson, 1968; Ourth & Brown, 1961; Robson, 1967; Robson & Moss, 1970; Sroufe & Waters, 1975; Stewart *et al.*, 1954; Wahler, 1967; Watson, 1965; Wolff, 1963; Yarrow, 1963; Zelazo, 1971.)

Effects of Paternal Behavior

Although fathers, when interviewed, usually consider themselves to be active participants in the daily care of their children, the infor-mation we have about their childcare role is exceedingly limited. Fathers have almost never been included in observational research, and when included in interview studies, their reports about what is going on in the home differ significantly from mothers'. As men are being increasingly encouraged to share the responsibilities of child care, this lack of knowledge becomes serious.

Information is particularly scarce concerning fathers' activities with infants. One recent survey shows that the amount of time fathers spend in *any* kind of household work varies from one to two hours a day (depending on how many hours they are employed). Another study, which recorded fathers' verbal behavior toward their infants, found the average amount of verbal interaction between father and infant was 37 seconds a day—and decreased from the time the infant was 2 weeks to 3 months old. Probably the total amount of father–infant interaction in most homes is somewhere between these esti-mates. Clearly, mothers and fathers are not comparable in the amounts of time they spend with their infants, and even in the mid-1970's, in most families, the primary responsibility for housework and child care rests with the wife and mother.

When fathers and infants have been observed together, however, whether or not the mother was present, fathers were very active. They held, rocked, and smiled at the baby more frequently than did mothers in these studies, and looked at, touched, and talked to the infant to the same degree the mothers did in an equal period of time. Although the amount of contact with the infant may have been inflated by the presence of an observer, this does indicate the willingness of fathers (from a variety of different educational and occupational levels studied) to participate in activities with infants. Moreover, as has already been suggested, in the first six months, before the infant forms a specific attachment to one person, it does not seem to matter to the infant who provides the stimulation and social contact. In fact, infants at this age respond identically to men and women.

There is no research evidence that biological mothers are more effective than adoptive mothers or that women are more effective than men in caring for infants and promoting their psychological development. Those who would argue that a lactating female is necessary are contradicted by evidence that milk from a bottle provides adequate nutrition, that bottle-fed babies do not suffer psychological harm, or that infant monkeys prefer a terry-cloth surrogate mother to a lactating wire model. Those who would use the monkeys' behavior to argue that women, being physically softer, give better care than men, would have to first prove that even the brawniest father is "made of steel"—that is, is equivalent to the wire monkey. It may indeed be that most women are better prepared than most men in our society for the nurturant role of parenting by virtue of their different socialization and biological condition and by social convention. But, as yet, there have been no systematic investigations that would prove that generalization is necessarily and inevitably true. Judging by the research on parent-infant interaction that is available, it seems likely that in the first six months, at least, fathers and mothers have a *parallel* influence on their infant's behavior, the relative extent of their influence being determined by the amount and quality of interaction each has with the infant. (Banikiotes *et al.*, 1972; Harlow, 1958, 1969; Nash, 1965; Parke, 1973; Parke *et al.*, 1972; Rebelsky & Hanks, 1971; Tasch, 1952; Walker, 1972.)

Early Childhood: Six Months to Three Years

"Depriving" Environments

Although during the first six months of life differences between children in institutional and home environments are small and reversible, there is a consensus among investigators who have studied older children in such depriving environments that children who spend the first one to three years in institutions that are perceptually barren and understaffed, that provide little opportunity for locomotion and no individualized care or attention, are significantly retarded. The extent of retardation is related to the magnitude of deprivation. In severely depriving environments, it is not uncommon to find the level of functioning impaired by as much as 30 or 40 IQ points. Retardation is often observed in cognitive and motor development, and almost inevitably in language and social relations. If locomotor opportunities and toys are available, motor skills develop satisfactorily. If the institution is brightly painted, well equipped with stimulating objects, and staffed by caretakers who have a knowledge of child development, the children are generally happy and of normal IQ, but their language and social adjustment scores are still low. When vocalization and social development of particular children are normal, it has been attributed to sustained individual attention from one or a few caretakers. For the normal development of social relations it appears that more is needed than physiological caretaking or perceptual stimulation; frequent and continuous interaction with the same adult caregivers is essential. (Ainsworth, 1962; Brodbeck & Irwin, 1946; Dennis, 1960; Dennis & Najarian, 1957; DuPan & Roth, 1955; Freud & Burlingham, 1944; Goldfarb, 1945; Kagan, 1968; Pringle & Bossio, 1960; Provence & Lipton, 1962; Rabin, 1958, 1964; Roudinesco & Appell, 1950; Saltz, 1973; Schenk-Danzinger, 1961; Spitz, 1946, 1965.)

Studies of differences related to socioeconomic status for this age period reveal significant variation in children's development, parents' behavior, family size and structure, and the physical environment of the home. Middle-class families tend to be smaller than families of low SES and are more likely to have both parents living at home; middle-class homes are less crowded, tend to be less noisy, and often contain more stimulating objects with which children may play. The attitudes middle-class mothers reveal in interviews tend to be more positive toward and accepting of children of this age than those expressed by poorer and less educated mothers—and these attitudes are reflected in maternal behavior. Although no difference related to socioeconomic status has been observed in the amount of time mothers and children spend together, middle-class mothers and children are more likely than their less affluent and educated counterparts to interact actively while they are together—at least under the watchful eye of a researcher. The most consistently noted differences are in the degree and quality of verbal interaction. In observational situations at home or in the laboratory, mothers with more education and higher social status are generally more verbal—both spontaneously and in response to the child's expressive behavior. Their speech is more "distinctive"—it occurs while the mother is face-to-face with the child and not otherwise occupied, and is uncontaminated by other noises such as that of the television set. It contains more questions and references to objects, fewer commands and rejecting statements, and is more complex and varied. These same mothers imitate their children more often and reward them more frequently, often verbally. They also play with their children more often and more affectionately and are more deliberately stimulating and didactic. They put fewer restrictions on the child's exploration and offer more toys and less TV. They respond more promptly and contingently to infants' frets and are more sensitive to what a fret might indicate. If they are in physical contact with the infant, they are more likely to use this proximity as an opportunity for further stimulation. They are less likely to punish the child physically, are less controlling, prohibitive, and intrusive, warmer, more understanding, and accepting. (Bayley & Schaefer, 1960b; Beckwith, 1972; Cazden, 1966; Kagan, 1968; Minton et al., 1971; Moss et al., 1969; Nelson, 1973; Schoggen, 1969; Tulkin, 1970; Tulkin & Cohler, 1973; Tulkin & Kagen, 1972; White, 1966; Williams & Scott, 1953.)

Far fewer differences related to socioeconomic status have been observed in children's behavior at this age than have been observed in their mothers. Differences in children's performance gradually increase with age, children in middle-class families becoming increasingly advanced. For *early* development of cognitive ability (development of relational and manipulative schemes and the concept of object permanence, for instance) the typical low-income family appears adequate or even advantageous. With later and more advanced cognitive measures (e.g., using objects as means to desired ends, using objects for their socially intended functions, solving problems, choosing more complex toys, and doing more complicated things with them) children from more affluent and better educated families do relatively better. On overall measures of IQ, 6- to 12-month-old infants of working-class parents score highest of any SES group. By 18 months, however, children in higher income families, as a group, score higher than children from lower-income families, and by 30 months, the mean scores of the three socioeconomic groups are significantly separated. By this age, too, children in families of higher socioeconomic status have been observed to play with toys more often and longer (in the laboratory as well as at home), to smile and vocalize to people more, to respond to meaningful speech and visual stimuli more maturely, and to be better able to use their mothers as resources.

We must caution, however, that these generalizations are based on average group differences—and indicate probable rather than necessary and inevitable relationships. Moreover, we must further caution that mean differences in children's IQ related to SES may reflect differences in genetic as well as environmental conditions. Although parental genotype and rearing environment typically covary in the population, some studies have found that children's IQ is more highly correlated with their natural mothers' IQ than with their adoptive mothers' social status. Clearly, socioeconomic status, *by itself*, accounts for a relatively small proportion of the variance in children's behavior and ability. (Beckwith, 1971a; Hindley, 1970; Honzik, 1967; Kagan, 1968; Messer & Lewis, 1972; Reppucci, 1971; Scarr-Salapatek, 1975; Tulkin, 1970; Wachs *et al.*, 1971; Willerman & Broman, 1970.)

Effects of Maternal Behavior

EFFECTS ON INTELLECTUAL COMPETENCE. The supreme value that American educators, researchers, and parents currently place on intelligence and intellectual achievement is amply demonstrated by the vast number of studies on environmental correlates of children's mental development in this and subsequent age periods. Innumerable studies are available which relate the child's intelligence to maternal behavior. Before these studies are summarized, it is relevant to remind the reader that intelligence, or intellectual competence, at this age represents a broad overall competence, the measurement of which is based on the child's ability to manipulate objects, to understand and speak language, to solve practical problems, and to cooperate with the examiner. Frequent criticisms of IQ tests and testing procedures have been raised recently, criticisms which apply to most of the studies reviewed here. When investigators have examined young children's self-directed, solitary intellectual activities, however, this kind of behavior has been very closely related to IQ test measures. It seems plausible, therefore, that IQ measures at this age do reflect quite adequately the complex intellectual competence or intelligence of young children.

A large number of researchers have focused on measures of children's IQ and related them to various aspects of maternal behavior. Those who have examined the relation between IQ and only one or two dimensions of maternal behavior seldom agree on which aspects of behavior are critical. In different studies, the child's IQ has been related to all of the following types of maternal behavior: discipline, "growth vocalization," psychological-mindedness, positive affective tone, hostile detachment (negatively), verbal stimulation, and physical contact. Investigators who have analyzed an array of variables simultaneously, however, suggest that just as IQ is defined by a cluster of infant skills, so maternal behaviors cluster to form a pattern of "optimal care." This syndrome of maternal behavior includes looking at, talking to, smiling at, playing with, and offering toys to the child—appropriately, effectively, nonrestrictively, and responsively. Research suggests that the child's most valuable intellectual experiences at this age occur in interaction with another person who teaches, helps, entertains, converses with, shares, and expands the child's activities. These kinds of maternal behavior are most closely related to children's overall competence.

The stimulation and responsive components of the syndrome of optimal care, moreover, have been linked causally with increases over time in the child's IQ and cognitive ability. In one study, over a 6-month period (from 12 to 18 months), increases of 5 to 20 points in individual children's IQ scores were observed to be the results of more attentive maternal behavior. In another study, from 12 to 24 months, the same kind of maternal behavior was found to lead to changes in children's sophistication of play, a reflection of cognitive ability assessed in nontest situations.

Of course, maternal behavior *alone* does not determine children's intelligence or cognitive ability. Such ability is related also to parental intelligence, through the mechanism of genetic inheritance. However, when attempts are made to separate the relative contributions to development of heredity and environment, it is clear that children's intellectual competence at this age is highly related to the mother's behavior as well as to her genotype. This is demonstrated by studies relating the intelligence of adopted children to that of their biological and their adoptive mothers; by studies comparing children raised by retarded mothers with the offspring of retarded fathers raised by normal mothers; and by research which analyzes statistical relations among the multiple variables of maternal behavior and intelligence and children's behavior and intelligence. In one such multivariate investigation, for example, the pattern of "optimal maternal care" which has been identified here accounted for 45% of the variance in children's overall competence, whereas maternal IQ accounted for only 7%. Clearly, the direct influence of maternal behavior on children's development is very powerful. One estimate of the extent of maternal behavior effects on the development of children's IQ is that the IQ of children raised by parents of low (less than 80) IQ can be increased by 25 points if they are reared under the best child-care conditions. Other estimates concur in suggesting that the reaction range of most IQ genotypes is probably ± 10 to 12 IQ points, in low- to high-average rearing conditions.

As some of the data on social class differences implied, it is possible for children to perform very well in test situations at this early age, and to have initially high IQ scores, if their mothers are negative, controlling, and intrusive. This appears to be particularly true for boys. (In fact, the intellectual development of boys seems consistently more susceptible to the influence of maternal behavior than does that of girls.) If, however, one measures IQ increment, or IQ at a later age, it is clear that positively stimulating maternal behavior to children at this age is more beneficial for intellectual development than negative and controlling behavior.

As well as initiating positive stimulating contact with the child, it is also beneficial, as we have suggested, if the mother responds to the child's attempts to initiate contact with her. During the first year of life, prompt responsiveness to the infant's cries of distress is important to development, but in the second and third years, responsiveness to distress becomes less significant (as fretting and crying become less frequent). At this age, prompt, appropriate, and contingent responses to gestural and vocal social expressions are more important for children's continued development. Such responsiveness does more than increase the frequency of the specific behaviors thus "reinforced." It significantly affects measures of overall competence and intelligence, presumably by increasing the child's motivation to enter new situations in which he anticipates that his behavior will also have predictable and positive consequences.

When components of intellectual competence are analyzed separately, the child's early skill with objects seems most closely related to the mother's provision of and play with a variety of play materials (more than to merely the number or variety of objects available in the home—as long as there are more than a minimal number). Only after the age of 2½ or so are the child's self-initiated interactions with the physical environment related to his intellectual competence. Children's exploration of the environment and lack of anxiety in new places and their willingness to play with novel objects is facilitated by an interesting environment and by the presence of a nonrestrictive mother with whom they have interacted frequently. (Ainsworth, 1969; Bayley, 1965; Bayley & Schaefer, 1964; Becker, 1964; Beckwith, 1971a; Bradshaw, 1968; Caldwell, 1967; Carew, 1975; Clarke-Stewart, 1973; Cox & Campbell, 1968; Engel & Wieder, 1971; Ferguson, 1971; Gordon et al., 1969; Honzik, 1957, 1967; Kessen et al., 1975; Ramey et al., 1971; Rheingold & Samuels, 1969; Scarr-Salapatek, 1975; Schaefer & Aaronson, 1972; Tulkin, 1970.)

Since the scientific study of child care began, there have been numerous attempts to intervene in situations where caretaking did not appear to be adequate. After the detrimental effects of institutionalization were first reported, investigators tried to enrich institutional environments in various ways. With children older than six months, the *most* effective intervention—in terms of permanently stemming retardation in all areas—appeared to be the provision of a substitute mother who provided attentive and responsive care and to whom the child could become attached. This was effective even if the substitute mother was herself mentally retarded. Recently, educational programs for children from "disadvantaged" homes have gained popularity. They have a similar aim. Based on the available results of such interventions with children under three years old, it may be concluded that such programs are able to effect significant increments in such groups. The magnitude and duration of relative intellectual gains varies in different studies (typically about 15 points for the group average) depending upon the kind of intervention. The effectiveness of programs for producing and maintaining IQ gains is greatest when the children are younger (though probably not younger than six months), when the curriculum is presented individually, usually in the home, over a longer period of time, and— perhaps most important—when the mother or other primary caregiver is explicitly involved in interacting in specified and stimulating ways with the child. (Bronfenbrenner, 1974; Fein & Clarke-Stewart, 1973; Gordon, 1969; Gordon et al., 1969; Horowitz & Paden, 1973; Karnes, 1969; Levenstein, 1970; Palmer, 1969; Rheingold & Bayley, 1959; Schaefer et al., 1968; Skeels et al., 1938; Skodak & Skeels, 1945; Weikart & Lambie, 1968.)

EFFECTS ON LANGUAGE ACQUISITION. The period from six months to three years witnesses the beginning of children's "real" speech: the first word (around a year), a vocabulary "explosion" (around 18 months), the first two-, three-, and four-word sentences (shortly thereafter). Until that time, the relation with maternal behavior described for infant vocalization holds: the frequency of vocalizing is increased by contingent audiovisual reinforcement or reciprocal adult vocalization. After the babbling stage, however, with the development of true language, there is no evidence that reinforcement aids the child's progress. Now it is adult-initiated verbal stimulation that is most important for the child's comprehension and production of language (particularly for size and richness of vocabulary and for the age at which multiword sentences are first produced). The amount, richness (variety), and complexity of adult speech in face-to-face interaction with the child is related to when, how early, and how well the child talks and understands speech. Adults' speech to children differs significantly from their speech to other adults; it is simpler, more redundant, more concrete, slower, and contains shorter sentences and more pauses. As the child begins to talk and his language ability increases, so does the complexity of speech directed toward him (even over a period of months). This seems to be an important factor in facilitating his further language acquisition. The child's development of language is also related to his cognitive development, and, consequently, to the factors described in the preceding section. Beyond this general relation, however, the clearest and most direct influence on the child's language ability at this age seems to be the speech of his language "models"—those persons who demonstrate adult language by talking to the child. The primary language model is usually the mother, but a variety of adults can also serve to enhance children's language development. Both the child's language skill and style of usage reflect the speech of his or her models. Early vocabulary and understanding of specific concepts are aided by the model's descriptive references to concrete objects with which the child is occupied, and by the use of questions. Once the child begins to talk, the match between his conceptual organization of the world and that of the adult who is the language model facilitates further development. The child makes proposals about the world and about words, and learns language from their acceptance or rejection. Naturally, if his concepts are similar to the model's he will experience more acceptances and fewer rejections. Language acquisition and use are facilitated by a nondirective, accepting, responsive, and elaborate adult speech strategy (one which accepts and expands on the child's verbal and nonverbal behavior) rather than by a critical, corrective, commanding mode. In the latter part of this age period, children's ability to produce grammatical sentences is related to the syntactic complexity of the model's speech. (Beckwith, 1971b; Buium et al., 1973; Cazden, 1966; Cazden et al., 1973; Clarke-Stewart, 1973; Dodd, 1972; Fowler & Swenson, 1975; Kessen et al., 1975; Nelson, 1973; Phillips, 1973; Snow, 1972; Starr, 1974; Tulkin, 1970; Ventis, undated.)

EFFECTS ON SOCIAL DEVELOPMENT. The most significant social development of childhood occurs near the beginning of this age period: the child forms his or her first emotional "attachment" to another person. He watches, follows, smiles at, and vocalizes to that person—significantly more than to any other; he often cries when she (or he) leaves, greets her happily upon her return, and clings to her when he is upset. If the child is separated from the person for a long period of time after this attachment has been formed, his behavior is anxious and depressed, even after their reunion. It has been suggested that this attachment forms the basis for all future social relationships, and that therefore its importance for social development cannot be overemphasized.

Almost all children develop some kind of attachment to someone in their first year of life. But a number of factors affect the intensity, the quality, the timing, and the target of that emotional bond. Individual differences observed in early infancy—in babies' social responsiveness, contact seeking, and fearfulness—constitute one such factor, which affects the quality of the attachment developed.

The "target" of the attachment bond, the attachment figure, on the other hand, is determined by how much an individual interacts with the infant in social and playful ways. Usually, but not always, in our society, the children's primary attachment is strongest to the mother or other primary caregiver. Typically, however, at the same time or soon after, the child also forms attachments to other salient social figures in his or her environment, such as the father or a sibling. (To simplify subsequent discussion, the attachment figure will hereafter usually be referred to as "mother".) The social interaction of the mother (or other attachment figure) with the child also affects the intensity of the attachment and its quality. It does not seem to depend solely on how much she is available or even around, or if there are other people involved in the child's physical care; it does not matter how much time she spends in caretaking activities or how skillful she is at them. It is the amount of time the mother spends in positive interaction with the child that is predictive of the intensity of the child's involvement. Although we know that an adequate amount of positive interaction with the mother is a necessary condition for attachment, however, exact hourly or daily limits for what is sufficient have yet to be established—and would undoubtedly vary from mother to mother and baby to baby.

The quality of the attachment relationship is reciprocal: when the mother gives optimal care (i.e., is attentive, affectionate, and responsive), the child develops an optimal pattern of attachment (is attentive, affectionate, and responsive to her). In an unfamiliar situation, or when presented with a new object, the child is able to leave the mother and explore. He does not need to maintain physical proximity or contact with her, as long as he can see her and return periodically for reassurance (especially when frustrated or afraid). His attachment behavior is balanced by his desire to explore; this pattern has been called "secure" attachment. Some children ignore the mother entirely; others hang on to her continuously. Examination of the experiences of these children shows that their mothers seldom interact with them, are not responsive to their needs and expressive behavior, and may be rejecting and hostile.

Evidence of the child's attachment increases in intensity from the time of the initial attachment relationship (around seven months) until sometime around 16 months. After that age the child gradually increases his independence from the primary attachment figure; first physically, then socially. Children who initially have been very physically dependent on their mothers tend to remain so. During the period of maximal attachment, the securely attached child may exhibit anxiety when confronted by an unfamiliar adult—especially if left alone with the stranger, if the stranger is intrusive, or if the child has not previously interacted with people other than his mother.

Although children in early childhood prefer their primary attachment figures, they often also develop significant social relationships with other people—in the extended family or in day care, for example. This does not impair the primary attachment relationships. As they get older and interact more with other people, children's social behavior tends to reflect the security of their earlier attachment and interactions with their parents. At two or three years of age, children whose relations with their mothers were—and still are—more positive, playful, and responsive, show somewhat more mature social behavior. In particular, they are more sensitive to the behavior and characteristics of unfamiliar persons than are children whose relations with their mothers are less adequate. For instance, they differentiate between adults with whom they have or have not interacted previously—acting more responsive and cooperative with those they have seen before. Attachment to the mother may not translate *directly* to interaction with strangers and other people. But there is evidence that on some more subtle level, the child's initial attachment relationship affects subsequent social behavior and development.

As we have suggested before, it is exceedingly difficult to separate the social behavior of mother and child or to determine whether it is the mother's influence or the child's that is shaping their interaction. Spontaneous and responsive social behaviors are highly correlated, for both mother and child. Yet it has often been assumed that the mother is the causal agent. Longitudinal research demonstrates that this is simply not so. Overall, the frequency of the child's positive social behavior to the mother (looking, smiling, vocalizing) seems to affect how much time mother and child spend together, and how responsive the mother is to the child's distress. The child's smile elicits the mother's—not just immediately, but over a period of months the frequency of maternal smiling increases. Children who smiled a lot at their mothers at 11 months, for example, were observed to have mothers who smiled at them more often at 16 months. Still, one cannot simply conclude that mother-child social interaction is determined solely by the infant's disposition to smile. Interaction is not only immediately reciprocal, but the direction of influence is reciprocal over time; first one then the other person influences the behavior of his or her partner. The mother's attention to the infant leads to his attachment to her, which in turn increases her attentiveness, and so on.

The frequency of young children's *negative* emotional behavior is also related to maternal care. By the end of the first year, the infant's cry reflects the history of his mother's responsiveness to his distress, more than it does constitutional factors such as irritability or soothability, the effectiveness of the mother's soothing, or the sheer amount of physical contact with the mother. The frequency of crying is negatively related to the promptness and responsiveness of the mother's soothing behavior and the tender quality of her physical care. Negative behavior (crying, fretting, behaving aggressively) is related also to the frequency of the mother's ignoring, rejecting, scolding, hitting, commanding, and restrictive holding.

In sum, the relationship formed in this age period between the child and the mother or other primary figure is a central and essential one in the child's social development. Mutual attachment evolves through their frequent playful, positive and reciprocal interaction. (Ainsworth, 1963, 1964, 1973; Ainsworth *et al.*, 1971, 1972; Antonovsky, 1959; Bayley & Schaefer, 1960a; Beckwith, 1972; Bell & Ainsworth, 1972; Bowlby, 1958; Caldwell *et al.*, 1963, 1969; Caldwell & Hersher, 1964; Clarke-Stewart, 1973, 1975; Collard, 1968; Fleener, 1973; Gewirtz & Gewirtz, 1965; Goldberg & Lewis, 1969; Heinstein, 1963; Moss *et al.*, 1969; Rheingold, 1956; Ricciuti & Poresky, 1973; Robertson, 1962; Robson, 1967; Robson *et al.*, 1969; Schaefer & Bayley, 1963; Schaffer, 1958; Schaffer & Emerson, 1964; Tulkin, 1970; Walters & Parke, 1965.)

Effects of Paternal Behavior

As little is known about father-child interaction in this age period as in infancy. We do know, however, that children behave toward both parents in ways that are more similar than different. Except during the "peak attachment" (12–18 months) they are equally willing to stay in a strange room or to interact with *either* parent. As the literature on attachment would predict, which parent is preferred during the 12- to 18-month period depends upon the quality and frequency of the parent's involvement with the child, rather than on who spends most time in routine physical caretaking. Since mothers are more frequently available and responsible for child care and thus have greater opportunity for developing involvements with their children, it is not surprising that although some children have been observed to form a primary attachment to the father, the majority become attached first to the mother. Before and after the "peak attachment" time when most children prefer to be with their mothers, infants of eight months and boys of five years have been observed to prefer *playing* with their fathers. This may be related to the observation that mothers and fathers differ qualitatively in their style of interacting with their children: mothers most often hold their children in order to perform caretaking functions while fathers hold them in the context of physical play. In families where there is a high degree of father-child interaction, moreover, it has been observed that children exhibit less anxiety when they are confronted by a stranger and perform better on tests of cognitive development. (High father involvement *may* be correlated with high mother involvement; there is no evidence on this point.) (Kotelchuck, 1973; Lamb, 1975; Lewis *et al.*, 1972; Schaffer & Emerson, 1964; Spelke *et al.*, 1973; Wachs *et al.*, 1971.)

Preschool: Three to Six Years

"Depriving" Environments

Although differences in *social* behavior such as cooperation and helping have not been observed, differences in the *intellectual* skills of children from families differing in economic resources and social and educational status are increasingly marked through the preschool period, extending the trends observed earlier. Differences between parents from different social strata seem relatively stable; they also reflect those observed earlier. In general, parents of higher socioeconomic status are higher on all measures of adult-initiated interaction related to the child's need for companionship, affection, and intellectual stimulation. Their methods and strictness of control also differ from those of parents at lower socioeconomic levels; they are more likely to request, consult, explain, rather than coax, command, threaten, and punish. However, caution must be applied in making generalizations from these observed differences. As we have pointed out before, studies of social class account for very little of the statistical variance in parent-child relations, and they often confound socioeconomic status with religion, race, geographical location, or ethnic origin—factors which have independent effects on parent–child relations. When child development is analyzed in terms of its relation to specific parental behavior rather than to broad socioeconomic categories, statistical relationships are generally more significant. Furthermore, it is not clear from studies of social class how much of the difference among parents is a function of material resources, how much is due to education, and how much is determined by biological differences. (Baumrind, 1972; Bee et al., 1969; Bronfenbrenner, 1958; Chilman, 1968; Dameron, 1955; Deutsch, 1973; Erlanger, 1974; Giovannoni & Billingsley, 1971; Havighurst & Davis, 1955; Herzog & Lewis, 1970; Hess, 1969; Hindley, 1970; Hunt, 1967; Kamii & Radin, 1967; Maccoby & Gibbs, 1953; Olim, 1970; Roy, 1950; Sears et al., 1957; Smart, 1964; Steward & Steward, 1973; Walters et al., 1964; Waters & Crandall, 1964; Wortis et al., 1963.)

Another sociological variable which differentiates families is the employment status of the mother. Although, until recently, mothers of children of preschool age have tended not to work, a number of past investigators have looked for possible effects of maternal employment on child development. No *consistent* differences between preschool children of working and nonworking mothers have been found, however, when potentially confounding variables (such as socioeconomic status, mother's age, child's age, mother's attitude toward working, stability of the home, presence of the father, and alternative child-care arrangements) have been controlled. This is not surprising, since one extensive survey reports that mothers spend almost the same amount of time in child care whether they are employed or not! One critical variable related to maternal care and child development seems to be whether the mother is *satisfied* with her role—be it housewife or career person. Employment status *per se* is unrelated to child-rearing patterns, but dissatisfied nonworking mothers (compared with satisfied working and nonworking and dissatisfied working mothers) report most difficulty in controlling their children, least enjoyment when with them, and least confidence as mothers—and are rated lowest on adequacy of mothering. Another important consideration is the quality of the substitute care: stable, stimulating substitute care is minimally essential for the child's psychological well-being. Finally, there is a suggestion that children who are under three years when their mothers begin work are more susceptible than older children to damaging effects of separation from mother and unstable or inadequate substitute care.

As the rate of mothers who work is climbing rapidly and steadily, it is becoming increasingly important to investigate the full range of potential effects of maternal employment on children's development. There are still many unanswered questions, and even the information we have needs updating to keep pace with changing social values, family roles, and available child-care services. (Ainsworth, 1973; Bronfenbrenner, 1975; Etaugh, 1974; Siegel *et al.*, 1959; Walker, 1972; Yarrow *et al.*, 1962.)

Effects of Maternal Behavior

INTELLECTUAL DEVELOPMENT.   The mother continues to influence the intellectual development of the child in the preschool period. If IQ is taken as a measure of intellectual ability, the child's development seems to be related to the following pattern of maternal behavior: (1) the mother is sensitive, warm, and loving toward the child (as she was when he was younger); (2) she generally accepts his behavior and allows him to explore and to express himself; (3) when she *does* exert control over his behavior, she uses reasoning or appeals to his feelings rather than imposing "rules"; (4) she is capable of, and uses, more sophisticated and elaborate language and teaching strategies; and, finally, (5) she pushes—she is concerned about the child's development and actively encourages his independence and stimulates his growth (by frequent reading, talking, teaching, and playing with toys). This pattern of maternal behavior is related not only to high IQ scores but to IQ *gains* made during the preschool period. Moreover, when particular cognitive skills (like reading readiness, classification, or concept sorting) are measured rather than IQ, the same overall relationship is found. Not surprisingly, though, the child's ability to sort objects into conceptual categories seems to be *most* closely related to the mother's use of abstract language. The mother's use of verbal abstraction is also related to measures of the child's "potential creativity"—the complexity and variety of play. Mothers of highly creative children also are more likely to enhance the "playfulness" of the home environment by providing novelty, variety, nonstereotyped toys, and opportunities for exploration. A relationship between the mother's stimulating behavior and the child's cognitive development exists in all families, but the relationship is particularly strong between mothers and sons.

Knowing the empirical relationship between maternal stimulation and children's development, investigators have attempted to enrich children's intellectual experiences by changing mothers' behavior. Such programs have had some success in increasing the IQ scores of preschool children from less than optimal home environments. While home-based parent education programs were found to be the most effective intervention for this purpose at younger ages, however, they have not been as effective in preparing children for school. The intervention strategy from three to six years which has been proposed as most likely to succeed is the gradual introduction of group preschool programs into ongoing home programs. Even at this age, though, the involvement of the parent is valuable. Parental education and involvement can support and enhance IQ gains made by children in preschool programs.

When one looks beyond IQ measures, some preschool children are observed to be significantly more competent overall in their interaction with the world. They are characterized as having a good "learning style." In preschool settings, they move about energetically, explore freely, and rely on their own initiative without repeated adult urging. They manipulate toys and observe the effects of their own actions; they order and control materials and events with reasonable independence of, but not alienation from, adults. They apparently have learned through interactions with their parents that the world is interesting, predictable, controllable, and nonthreatening. They have learned what aspects of the environment are relevant, what actions are permitted—and have been given a wide range of each.

In sum, mothers' rules, expectations, prohibitions, attitudes—clearly expressed in interaction with their children—significantly affect children's intellectual competence, whether such competence is measured by standardized test or clinical observation. Children's development is enhanced by maternal behavior that is both stimulating and accepting. (Baldwin *et al.*, 1945; Baumrind, 1971a; Baumrind & Black, 1967; Bayley, 1965; Bayley & Schaefer, 1964; Bishop & Chace, 1971; Bresnahan & Blum, 1971; Bronfenbrenner, 1974; Costello & Martin, 1971; Costello & Peyton, 1973; Hess & Shipman, 1967; Hurley, 1959; Karnes, 1969; King, 1966; LaFore, 1945; Moss & Kagan, 1958; Olim, 1970; Radin, 1971, 1972b.)

EFFECTS ON LANGUAGE DEVELOPMENT.   A limited body of research suggests that children's language competence and usage in the preschool period continue to reflect characteristics of the verbal environment. Their language ability is related to the amount of adult speech to the child (talking and reading) but not to the total amount of speech in the environment. It is related to the acceptance, relevance, and informational content of this speech (answering questions, reading stories, teaching rhymes, labeling objects, and not giving negative commands). (Holzman, 1969; Marshall, 1961; Tizard *et al.*, 1972.)

EFFECTS ON SOCIAL DEVELOPMENT.   In the period from three to six years, children increasingly "detach" themselves from their mothers; they become more autonomous; and they intensify and increase the scope of their relationships with other children. Because of its relevance to both theory and practice (i.e., nursery school management), the study of the child's social behavior at this age has been very popular. The complex array of information gathered in innumerable studies since the 1930's can be overwhelming. Sorting out mature from immature dependency, boys from girls, mothers from fathers, to mention a few dimensions, is exceedingly complicated. Consequently, the information has been summarized in tabular form (Table I). The major problem in integrating this large and diffuse literature arises in combining variables from different studies—variables that were measured in different ways, in different situations with different subjects. Nevertheless, after considerable distillation of the data, some general, relatively consistent, and recurrent relationships appear. They are presented in the table and highlighted below. Lack of clarity is still noticeable on some dimensions—especially when child behavior is ambiguous, broad, or variously defined, as, for example, "masculinity" and "femininity." Results are clearest on positive aspects of children's social behavior.

In general, this research on social development reveals once more how different aspects of parental behavior interact in producing an effect on children's behavior. The effect of the parents' mode of discipline, to give one very clear example, cannot be separated from the emotional context in which it occurs. Parental discipline which sets definite limits on children's behavior, and which exerts a relatively high degree of control firmly and consistently, but also gently and in a positive emotional context, is one pattern of parental behavior which seems to be related to children's social development. These parents

Table I

Social Behavior of the Preschool Child
and Related Parental Factors

| Child's Behavior | | Parents' Behavior[a] | | | |
	Emotional	Disciplinary	Stimulating	Responsive	Quantity
1. *Immature dependency* (seeking physical proximity and help, low self-control)	No consistent relation	In infancy, M[b] was restrictive, frustrating, punitive In preschool, M is permissive, indulgent, not severely frustrating or punitive; F is lax, ineffectual, or ambivalent	No pressure or demands for maturity; "infantilization" of child	M is generally nonresponsive and rewards dependent behavior	F is absent and M is only caretaking person
2. *Mature dependency* (seeking attention, approval, and affection)	Boys: M,F are rejecting Girls: M,F are warm	Boys: F is strict Girls: M, F are permissive, use love-withholding discipline	Boys: No relation Girls: M pressures for independence	Boys: F does not reward dependency Girls: F rewards dependency	Boys: F does not spend time with child Girls: No relation

Behavior					
3. *Independence* (assertive, purposive, achievement-oriented behavior)	Boys: M,F are warm, affectionate, approving; Girls: M is warm, affectionate, approving; F may be detached	Parents enforce rules firmly and consistently Boys: M,F are democratic, authoritative or permissive, and nonconforming Girls: M is democratic, authoritative, permissive, or "harmonious"; F is punitive	M,F are demanding (of age-appropriate behavior), pressuring, accelerating, treat child like adult	M,F reward mature, independent achievement, are responsive, helpful, encourage and satisfy child's need for information	No data
4. *Dominance* (directing, domineering, defying)	No data	Boys: M is strict; Girls: F is strict	M demands controls, achievement, self-sufficiency, order	No data	No data
5. *Aggression* (hostility, disobedience, aggressive pretend play)	M,F are hostile	M,F are directive, dictating, interfering, restrictive, nonaccepting, punitive,	No data; probably no relation	M,F are generally not responsive; they reward aggression	F or older brother is present

(continued)

Table I (continued)

Child's Behavior	Parents' Behavior[a]				
	Emotional	Disciplinary	Stimulating	Responsive	Quantity
5. *Aggression* (hostility, disobedience, aggressive pretend play) (*continued*)		especially for aggression. Use unqualified power-assertion not love-with-holding discipline. If long and severe may result in inhibition of *overt* aggression, especially in girls			
6. *Social withdrawal* (avoidance of people, self-aggression)	M (of girls), F (of boys) is rejecting or detached	M or F is non-accepting, punitive, authoritarian, and may be restrictive	No data; probably no relation	M,F respond negatively to C's behavior	No data

7. *Sociability* (warm, cooperative, concerned, outgoing interaction)	M,F are warm, especially for girls	M,F are authoritative or permissive—not authoritarian; discipline is consistent and other-oriented, especially for boys	M models positive social behavior	M rewards co-operation, is generally responsive	No data
8. *"Masculine" behavior*	F is warm	Boys: F is dominant and may be punitive Girls: F is dominant and permissive	Boys: F is masculine	Girls: F rewards dependency	Girls: F is active caretaker
9. *"Feminine" behavior*	M is warm	M is dominant, restrictive, and punitive, especially of aggression	Boys: M socializes severely and pressures for independence	Boys: M is responsive Girls: M rewards dependency	Boys: F is absent

[a] Unless otherwise specified, parental behavior is concurrent with child's behavior, i.e., occurs in the preschool period.
[b] The abbreviations "M" and "F" refer to "Mother" and "Father," respectively.

behave in a way that is warm yet authoritative; they emphasize the "do's" (prescriptions) more than the "don'ts" (proscriptions). This pattern of "authoritative" discipline differs from both "permissive" discipline—in which there are no or very few limits—and "authoritarian" discipline—in which rules are many, restrictive, arbitrary, and strictly enforced. "Harmonious" discipline is another pattern of parental behavior, in which parents do not visibly exercise control, but focus on achieving harmony within the family; they are very accepting, encourage the child's independence, and treat him or her as they would an adult.

Patterns of authoritative and harmonious discipline have been associated with a pattern of particularly mature and competent social behavior in children. These children exhibit both independence *and* sociability. When observed at home or in nursery school, they appear self-confident, assertive, and autonomous, and yet they are also friendly and do conform, when appropriate, to group standards. They are considerate to other people, helpful, nurturant, sympathetic, and generous. Parental behaviors which are especially closely related to the sociability end of this pattern of social competence, i.e., warm, cooperative, gregarious behavior, model and reward such positive social behavior in their children. Parental behaviors related to the independence aspect, i.e., purposive, achievement-oriented behavior, demand and reinforce their children's autonomous, mature (age-appropriate) achievement and behavior.

Parents who are authoritarian and hostile, by contrast, are more likely to have children who are aggressive, hostile, and disobedient. The parents' hostile restriction and frustration of the child's activities leads to anger in the child; the parents' physical punishment provides the child with a model of aggressive behavior. Permissive parents are more likely to have immature, dependent children.

The research on relations between parental behavior and children's social characteristics also suggests a complex interaction of maternal and paternal roles and differential effects of those roles on boys and girls. It is clear that neither parent alone accounts for the child's development. When each parent behaves in markedly different ways, it seems to lead to the less desirable patterns of children's social behavior such as dependency and immaturity, or to less significant aspects of children's behavior such as stereotyped masculine or feminine role behavior. Children are most likely to be competent when the behavior of *both* parents is characterized by the qualities of love, respect, and moderate control. (Baldwin, 1949; Baldwin *et al.*, 1945; Bandura *et al.*, 1963; Baumrind, 1965, 1966, 1967, 1971a,b; Baumrind & Black, 1967; Bayley & Schaefer, 1960a; Becker, 1964; Becker *et al.*, 1962; Biller, 1969; Bishop, 1951; Brody, 1969; Bryan, 1975; Crandall *et al.*, 1958, 1960; Hatfield *et al.*, 1967; Heathers, 1951; Hess & Handel, 1956; Hetherington, 1965; Hetherington & Frankie, 1967; Highberger, 1955, 1956; Hoffman, 1960, 1963; Korner, 1949; LaFore, 1945; Levin & Sears, 1956; Martin, 1975; Mummery, 1954; Mussen & Parker, 1965; Olejnik & McKinney, 1973; Rutherford & Mussen, 1968; Santrock, 1970; Schaefer & Bayley, 1963; Sears, 1966; Sears *et al.*, 1953; Trapp & Kausler, 1958; Wimberger & Kogan, 1972; Venar, 1966; Wittenborn, 1956, 1957; Yarrow *et al.*, 1973.)

Effects of Paternal Behavior

Fathers and mothers have been repeatedly observed to differ in their treatment of preschool children. Mothers tend to be more expressive, nurturant, rewarding, responsive, playful, accepting, and verbal with children of either sex (although there is a tendency for them to be somewhat more controlling with girls). Fathers are more likely to be distant, instrumental, physical, and demanding—particularly with their sons. It follows that (in a one-to-one interaction in a structured situation) children are more task oriented with their fathers and more socially involved with their mothers. It also follows that the commonly observed sex-based difference in children's achievement (independent of ability) is fostered by a family milieu in which encouragement and modeling of achievement (by fathers) is strongest for sons. Differences between maternal and paternal roles and behavior seem to be diminishing (and currently are smaller in families in which parents are more educated), but are still relevant in the 1970's. Moreover, since research suggests that it is fathers who differentiate most sharply in their treatment of boys and girls, differences are likely to persist—at least until the feminist movement focuses more determinedly and effectively on changing *men's* attitudes.

The effects of fathers—or, more often, of fathers' absence—on the behavior of preschool children has received attention from investigators in the past. Particular interest has been shown in effects on *boys'* development. If the father is absent for a prolonged period, especially before the child is four or five years old, preschool boys tend to be less aggressive and more dependent on their mothers and other people. They have also been observed to be more demanding and compulsively obedient than boys with fathers present. However, it is not just the absence of the father *per se* that is responsible. On the one hand, boys' dependency may occur when the father lives at home but is functionally absent or ineffectual. On the other hand, when the father is away, the behavior of the mother is relevant. If the mother is the sole caretaker and if she behaves overprotectively, this fosters the child's dependency. If, however, she supports and encourages the child's independence from her, there need be no development of overdependency. The presence of a father substitute also can alleviate overdependency. If the father or father substitute is very aggressive and punitive (especially if he behaves toward the mother in an aggressive way) the boy will tend to be more aggressive. Studies have found that boys develop the most satisfactory masculine sex role if they have a close relationship with a warm, effective, authoritative and relatively dominant father. As would be expected from the study of mother–child relations, the quality of the father–son relationship is more important than merely the amount of time the two spend together. The facilitating effect of sons' interaction with their fathers applies not only to sex role and social development, but to performance on cognitive tests and achievement motivation as well. A firm and demanding, yet loving, father seems to enhance the son's cognitive development. Boys' intellectual development is hindered by a family situation in which the mother is *markedly* warmer or more dominant than the father.

Far less research has probed the effects of paternal absence or behavior on the psychological development of *girls*. The research that is available suggests that the absence of the father apparently does not affect girls' social development, although it may be detrimental to their cognitive development. If the father is the more dominant parent, participates extensively in the care of the child, and is very affectionate toward her, the daughter is more likely to imitate characteristics and behaviors of the father, and be a "daddy's girl." This is especially true if the mother is not as affectionate as the father and actively pushes the girl toward independence.

At least in the area of social relations, and possibly for achievement as well, the key to optimal development for boys and girls seems to be a *balance* between the roles and behaviors of mother and father. If either parent, but particularly the opposite-sexed parent, is markedly more affectionate, dominant, or demanding than the other, the child's development may suffer. Extreme domination by either parent has been related to lower intellectual achievement for both boys and girls, and extreme domination or excessive affection by the opposite-sexed parent to problems in children's development of sex-role identity. In one-parent families, the danger that the only parent will be too dominating or affectionate can be alleviated by participation in child care by an opposite-sexed parent-figure. (Bandura et al., 1963; Baumrind & Black, 1967; Bell, 1965; Benson, 1968; Biller, 1968, 1969, 1970, 1971; Bronfenbrenner, 1961; Eron et al., 1961; Freeberg & Payne, 1967; Herzog & Lewis, 1970; Hetherington, 1965, 1967; Hoffman, 1971; Johnson, 1963; Laosa & Brophy, 1972; Levin & Sears, 1956; Osofsky & O'Connell, 1972; Parson & Bales, 1955; Radin, 1972, 1973; Rothbart, 1973; Rutherford & Mussen, 1968; Santrock, 1970; Sears, 1951; Stolz, 1954; Trapp & Kausler, 1958; Wohlford et al., 1971; Wyer, 1965.)

Family Size and Composition

Effects of parents' behavior on children's development are further complicated by the presence of siblings: number, sex, and birth order of siblings have all been correlated with various characteristics of the child. Presumably siblings affect the child both directly (by their behavior) and indirectly (by affecting parents' behavior). Unfortunately, the process of that influence is not entirely clear, since most research has been based merely on correlations between birth order and performance, rather than on observation of children of different ordinal position interacting with parents and/or siblings.

It has been reliably observed that first-born and only children of preschool age are generally advanced in verbal and intellectual skills—at least until another sibling is born. First-borns have also been observed to be less self-confident, socially outgoing, popular, and aggressive, and more emotional, suggestible, and dependent than only children or later-borns at this age. As infants, first-borns are given more attention and affection and interact more with their parents; but when another child is born, parental attention is withdrawn, and the first-born children experience less affectionate interaction with parents than do only children or later-borns of the same age. Parents are also more restrictive, coercive (especially the father), and inconsistent, more dependent on external resources (i.e., are more likely to try to bring up the child "by the book"), and less effective with first-borns. These characteristics are likely related to the dependent, insecure personality which has been observed in some first-born children. Parents are generally also more demanding and involved with the first child; in fact, they tend to talk to all their children at the level of the first-born's language ability. This behavior may be responsible for the accelerated verbal and intellectual development of the first-born child. Parents have less time for later-born children, for talking and playing and stimulating the infant, and they tend to be more accepting and relaxed about the child's development. This trend becomes more marked as family size increases—sometimes, in large families with closely spaced children to the point of inadequate care.

It has been suggested that first-born and only children are more like their parents, and that later-borns show greater variability. This raises the issue of the siblings' *direct* effects on child development. When spacing and sex of siblings, as well as number and order, are examined, extremely complex interactions result. The spacing and sex of siblings seem to be as important determinants of the child's characteristics as sex and birth order of the child himself. Investigations of these sibling variables suggests the following conclusions: (1) The less the age space between siblings, the greater is the siblings' influence; the greater the age space, the more the influence of the parent. (2) A two- to four-year space is most stressful and stimulating. (3) Having a sibling of the opposite sex is more stimulating than having one of the same sex. In general, children with opposite-sexed siblings are more cheerful, kind, and curious and exhibit more of the characteristics of the opposite sex (especially the young sibs). For example, a boy with an older sister is more withdrawn and dependent than a boy with an older brother; girls with brothers score higher than those with sisters on measures of mental abilities, verbal articulateness, ambition, competition, and decisiveness.

In sum, children's development seems to be related to the size and composition of the family, and the individual child's development to his or her place in the family structure. Both direct influences of siblings on each other and indirect effects of number and order of children on parental behavior have been suggested to account for the complex relations observed. (Bossard & Boll, 1966; Brim, 1958; Clausen, 1966; Fauls & Smith, 1956; Freeberg & Payne, 1957; Gewirtz & Gewirtz, 1965; Giovannoni & Billingsley, 1971; Goodenough & Leahy, 1927; Handolin & Gross, 1959; Hindley, 1970; Hurley & Hohn, 1971; Kessen *et al.*, 1975; Koch, 1955a,b, 1956a,b,c; Laosa & Brophy,

1972; Lasko, 1954; Levin & Sears, 1956; Minturn & Lambert, 1964; Nelson, 1973; Nisbet, 1953a,b; Rothbart, 1973; Santrock, 1970; P. Sears, 1951; R. Sears, 1950; Thoman *et al.*, 1970, 1972, 1973; Waldrop & Bell, 1964.)

The Early School Years: Six to Nine Years

"Depriving" Environments

It is in the area of school achievement that children from more affluent and educated families have most consistently been observed to surpass the performance of children from relatively poorer homes. This difference is undoubtedly related to parental values and behaviors which influence children's intellectual development and achievement motivation. Having assimilated the achievement-oriented values of a technological society, and often having succeeded in that society by virtue of their intellectual skills, middle-class and professional-class parents are more likely to reinforce their children's achievement and to criticize failure consistently and effectively. They have higher academic expectations for their children; they talk and read to the children more. They are more likely to stress goals for their children such as curiosity, consideration, and self-control, rather than obedience, neatness, and cleanliness.

These types of parental behavior and values are, without question, only partially responsible for observed differences in children's performance in school. Children's behavior is also affected by the larger society—by cultural and religious values of their immediate community, by the economic resources and, consequently, the nutrition and educational materials available to the family, by prejudice and discrimination from other groups in society, by the lack of predictability in unstable homes in a mobile society, and by parental depression and feelings of helplessness which result from coping with this world. Unfortunately research has not explored the effects of these conditions on children's development.

Research that examines the effects of working mothers' on school-aged children demonstrates once again that employment status is not a simple dimension. Not surprisingly, working mothers of school-aged children generally have higher *self-acceptance* than nonworking mothers, but are more likely to doubt their adequacy as mothers. The employment of the mother does not seem to hinder the child's school achievement; if the family is stable, it may even enhance it. If there *is* a negative effect of the mother's working, it is that it may increase boys' dependency. As we have seen before, however, the mother's satisfaction with her work status may be more relevant than the fact that she does or does not work. During the early school years satisfaction seems particularly related to the child's social behavior. Mothers who work—and dislike it—are less involved with their children; their children while often independent and assertive, are also frequently hostile. Children whose mothers enjoy working (and who tend to be warmer and less strict) are related higher in self-worth and personal adjustment. If the mother has successfully combined family and career, her children seem to have more "liberated" notions about work, sex roles, men and women. They perceive men and women as sharing more and being more similar. They judge women more competent and men warmer; they are more likely to think that work is suitable for women; and the girls are more likely to want and expect careers for themselves later on. The supervision of the child while the mother is working is also relevant—particularly to the child's intellectual development. Unsupervised children (who are almost inevitably from low-income families) tend to experience much greater cognitive impoverishment than those who are supervised. (Banducci, 1967; Etaugh, 1974; Hess, 1969; Hieronymus, 1951; Hoffman, 1961; Kohn, 1959; Nye & Hoffman, 1963; Poznanski *et al.*, 1970; Stolz, 1960; Weinberg, 1964; Woods, 1972.)

Effects of Maternal Behavior

EFFECTS ON INTELLECTUAL DEVELOPMENT AND SCHOOL ACHIEVEMENT.   Research on cognitive and language development in the early school years supports the evidence presented regarding children's development in the preschool period. Verbal ability, which at this age includes skill in reading as well as speaking and understanding oral language, is related to earlier interest and stimulation by the mother—amount of play, responses to early questions, reading, tutoring, and frequency of outings. Nonverbal intellectual ability is related to the physical materials that the mother provided during the early years, along with the freedom she allowed the child to explore them, and to the availability of toys and educational materials at the present age. The intellectual development of boys continues to be positively related to a close mother–son relationship throughout childhood. The same is not true for girls, however; research suggests that their superior intellectual performance is associated with a progressively more distant mother–daughter relationship. The inference to be drawn from the research is probably *not* that a cold mother produces a smart daughter—or even that a smart daughter makes the mother progressively more distant—although these explanations cannot be ruled out. What seems more likely is that in the past when this research was conducted, in an era when mothers were not likely to be working, a very close mother–daughter relationship could lead, through the daughter's strong identification with the nonworking mother, to a sex-stereotyped, domestic role for the girl—a role that might discourage exploration of the physical environment and manipulation of intellectual ideas. Thus the daughter who was close to, and like, her mother would not do as well in tests of intellectual achievement.

A critical issue raised for the first time in this school-age period is that of academic achievement. Achievement and intelligence are highly correlated, and, not surprisingly, are related to a similar pattern of home variables. However, children are often considered "overachievers" or "underachievers" in school, relative to their tested ability. When IQ and achievement are thus separated, there seems to be one type of parental behavior that most clearly and consistently predicts success in school—that is, the parents' *demands* for achievement. The parents of overachievers have, for themselves and their children, achievement standards which are high and explicit. Their behavior toward their children is authoritarian. When the child was younger, they were most likely controlling and restrictive; at this age they are still controlling, but now they begin to press for the child's independence and self-reliance. Finally, in these families, educational achievement is valued, expected, rewarded, and deliberately stimulated by teaching, academic guidance, family intellectuality, and modeling of structured work habits.

Whether or not the academic achievement of children in traditional school classes (which is where these studies were conducted) is desirable, or whether children's achievement behavior would transfer to nontraditional school settings, are open questions. There is some indication that certain characteristics of competence that are important for success in nontraditional "open" classes—such as creativity, curiosity, internal motivation for achievement, and lack of distractibility—are *not* related to authoritarian control and parental achievement demands. They may even be related to quite opposite parental behavior.

The following empirical generalizations follow from research on the latter kinds of behavior. Children's achievement *motivation* (as opposed to performance) seems to be related to early independence from parents. The ability to ignore distractions is predicted by parental behavior which is responsive and encouraging but does not provide specific directions and suggestions; ability to ignore misleading stimuli is negatively related to authoritarian parental behaviors such as controlling, directing, stressing conformity, and pushing the child toward parent-set goals and standards. Creativity, similarly, is negatively related to parental authoritarianism. Children who exhibit more curiosity about their surroundings have mothers who are more positive and attentive and less restrictive. In addition, a child's belief in his own ability to control his environment is related to warm, rewarding, and supportive parental behavior. Finally, if later achievement is the goal, getting into college may be related to early parental control, but high achievement standards in college are facilitated by early parental nurturance.

Clearly, these generalizations suggest that success in academic situations that call for innovative, independent, self-initiated, and determined work will not follow from the same pattern of controlling and demanding parental behavior that has been observed to enhance traditional school performance. If the methods of schooling and standards for success in school change in the direction of greater openness, so will parental behavior have to change in order to facilitate children's academic performance. The most effective pattern of behavior, then, for facilitating children's success in school, as well as their intellectual development, is likely to be nurturant but not restrictive, stimulating but not directive, responsive but not controlling, supportive of the child's independence but not demanding it. In general the parent's role for children of this age would be to provide an interesting, stimulating, safe environment—and to support the child's independent exploration of that environment. (Bayley & Schaefer, 1964; Becker *et al.*, 1959; Bee, 1967; Bing, 1963; Chance, 1961; Crandall *et al.*, 1964; Dave, 1963; Drews & Teahan, 1957; Heilbrun *et al.*, 1967; Hess, 1969; Honzik, 1967; Katkovsky *et al.*, 1967; Milner,

1951; Moss & Kagan, 1958; Nichols, 1964; Rosen & D'Andrade, 1959; Saxe & Stollak, 1971; Seder, 1957; Shaw, 1964; Winterbottom, 1958.)

EFFECTS ON SOCIAL DEVELOPMENT. Social behavior in the early school years parallels that in the previous three years, and the relations observed between maternal and child behavior still hold. The aggression of the eight-year-old, like that of the five-year-old, is related to parents' hostile, coercive, and physically punitive behavior. Parental rejection and restriction or protection, once again, are related to children's overdependency. Social withdrawal occurs when parents are punitive and unaffectionate. In contrast to the development of these negative social behaviors, prosocial behavior is fostered by mothers who are positive, attentive, accepting, and who reward cooperative behavior. (For girls who were highly prosocial, however, mothers were observed to be not overly affectionate—thus paralleling the trend noted for girls' intellectual development to benefit from a more distant mother–daughter relationship.) Self-confidence, self-esteem and self-assertion are related to a familiar pattern of parental behavior: parents who are themselves self-confident and harmonious, attentive and accepting, respect the individual freedom of the child, yet enforce clearly defined, rational, and appropriate limits. The development of conscience, which occurs during the school years (e.g., self-control and resistance to temptation), seems to be facilitated by maternal warmth and nurturance in combination with socialization pressure, and with parent–child discussions after the child breaks a rule. (Bayley & Schaefer, 1960a; Bronson, 1966; Coopersmith, 1967; Crandall et al., 1958; Finney, 1961; Hoffman et al., 1960; Kagan & Moss, 1962; Lefkowitz et al., 1963; McCord et al., 1962; Saxe & Stollak, 1971; Siegelman, 1966.)

To supplement generalizations from the foregoing research on maternal behavior, we may turn to another line of research—experimental research on children's prosocial behavior. The paradigm most often used in such research consists of observing children in a contrived (laboratory) situation after some experimental manipulation involving the performance of a model (typically an unfamiliar, adult female) who behaves in a way clearly specified by the experimenter. While not directly descriptive of parent–child relations, such research, by experimentally "testing" observed or theoretical parent–child relationships, does have indirect relevance—as long as we are justified in generalizing from an experimental model to a parent.

Briefly, the experimental research demonstrates that most children are more likely to exhibit prosocial behavior (altruistic, self-sacrificing, generous, helpful, or cooperative behavior) under the following circumstances: when such behavior is first performed by a model; the model is attentive, kind, affectionate, and rewarding; the model practices prosocial acts, but does not necessarily preach moral behavior or remind the child of social norms; the model has control over resources in the situation; the model appears to enjoy her own prosocial acts; the model uses inductive reasoning and talks about the consequences of the child's behavior; and when the experimental situation is characterized by positive affect and success for the child.

While it must be stressed that these generalizations are based on relatively short-term effects in an artificial situation, they are in basic agreement with results of studies of parent-child relations, and may be used, thus, to bolster explanations of child development in the family. One might suggest, then, that children's prosocial behavior is likely to be fostered in a family in which parents happily demonstrate and reward prosocial acts; in which parents are powerful and demand of the child certain social responsibilities—they set firm limits and standards for the child's moral and social behavior; and yet in which parents are basically accepting of the child—they are kind and loving and use reason to justify their limits and standards (cf. Bryan, 1975; Rosenhan, 1972).

Effects of Paternal Behavior

Detrimental effects of father absence on cognitive development, academic achievement, development of conscience, sex-role orientation, and social relations during the early school years have been observed repeatedly, but not consistently. The problem lies in the difficulty of separating the impact of the father's absence from associated factors such as the family's income and social acceptability, the reasons for, length, and type of fatherlessness, the presence of a stepfather, and the effect of the father's absence on the mother's attitudes and behavior. For example, although there seems to be some consensus that divorce is more strongly associated with adverse effects than is death of the father, it is not known whether this is because divorce creates friction and disorganization, or because death leads to relatively higher income, security, and social acceptability or to the creation of a mythical father-figure who is a paragon of fatherhood. When the father's absence is due to separation, divorce, or desertion, deficits occur most regularly when the absence occurs in the first five years of the child's life, and are most marked for boys; if the father's absence is due to death, detrimental effects are most likely for children over five years of age (most between six and nine years). The most general conclusion that can be drawn from studies of fatherless families is that paternal absence seems to be a contributory but not primary factor in depressing development.

Research on intact two-parent families also suggests that the degree to which the father is available is related to children's early academic achievement. Children whose fathers are home more than two hours a day are academically superior to those whose fathers are home less than one hour a day. But confounding variables undoubtedly also influence this relation. More meaningful comparisons would involve measures of the father's activities in the home. When such comparisons are made, children whose fathers are more accepting and nurturant, and actively teach the child, do better on IQ tests. As we have seen, the relationship between the son's IQ and his mother's behavior is very strong throughout childhood, but in the school years the direct impact of the father as a model of achievement and success becomes evident. In fact, one measure of boys' cognitive ability at this age, flexible thinking, is more closely related to paternal love, verbal stimulation, and power than to any maternal variables. Girls' achievement and cognitive development in the school years are also related to the father's behavior, particularly to his friendliness to her and to her mother. It is clear that both parents play a role in stimulating children's intellectual performance.

The behavior of both parents also influences the child's development of masculine or feminine identity. It has long been thought that lack of a father or of a resident male is a crucial element in the development of boys' masculine identity. However, review of the literature does not suggest that the absence of a father *necessarily* impairs masculine identity. The father is not the only source of masculine identity; peers and adult friends and relatives, as well as the media, can provide male models. In intact families, children at this age tend to prefer the sex role of the same-sexed parent, so long as they perceive that parent as warm, affectionate, and reasonably powerful. For girls, the father as well as the mother have an influence on sex-role development. The daughter's femininity is related to the father's adequacy, masculinity, consistency of discipline, encouragement of her participation in feminine activities, and his compatibility with the mother. It has also been observed that appropriate sex-role development of both boys and girls is related to paternal dominance. That is, in families in which the mother is markedly dominant, children have difficulty establishing their sex-role identity. This finding cannot be reduced to a generalization that maternal dominance is detrimental to children's development, however, since it was based on research in American families in which the *norm* was one of father dominance. A caution must be appended to all discussions of sex-role identity, at this time, since changing conceptions of "appropriate" male and female roles make much of the research on sex-role development outmoded. (Becker *et al.*, 1959; Biller, 1968, 1970; Biller & Weiss, 1970; Blanchard & Biller, 1971; Burton, 1972; Busse, 1969; Clausen, 1966; Corah, 1965; Cortes & Fleming, 1968; Hetherington, 1965, 1966; Herzog & Sudia, 1973; Hoffman, 1971; Honzik, 1967; Katkovsky *et al.*, 1967; Landy *et al.*, 1969; Lynn & Sawrey, 1959; Mitchell & Wilson, 1967; Mussen & Distler, 1960; Mussen & Rutherford, 1963; Mutimer *et al.*, 1966; Payne & Mussen, 1956; Radin, 1973; Santrock, 1972; Seder, 1957; Stendler, 1954; Sutton-Smith *et al.*, 1968.)

Siblings

The correlation of birth order with academic achievement is remarkably consistent: on measures of reading, verbal ability, school grades, achievement motivation, and task orientation, first-born and only children are markedly superior. Even when economic and physiological variables are taken into account, the relation between birth order or family size and intellectual achievement holds up. Although they frequently score higher on IQ tests as well, it has been suggested that the advantage of first-borns is primarily verbal and motivational. If the second sibling is born within three years of the first, and particularly if of the opposite sex, the first-born's IQ is lower (probably the result of less early parental stimulation), but achievement is higher (the result of earlier independence and autonomy, earlier competition for attention and approval, and earlier parental demands). Moreover, when the second child is born that soon, *his* verbal scores are even lower than his older sibling's. This underscores the importance of one-to-one parent-child interaction, which occurs less frequently when siblings are close in age.

First-borns, as school-aged children or adults, may be assertive and self-confident, or, more likely, dependent and fearful—the research evidence is not completely consistent on this point—but they are nearly always less sociable and less popular with their peers than later-born siblings. This may be because later-borns are brought up in a more relaxed atmosphere in which they experience earlier and more frequent interaction with other children. The effect of siblings is also observed in the area of sex-role development. Further support for our previous generalization that children are directly influenced by their siblings and grow more like them by imitation, modeling, and sharing activities and resources is that boys with brothers have higher masculinity scores and girls with sisters higher femininity scores. In general, it appears that siblings affect the child's cognitive development and academic achievement indirectly through their influence on parental behavior and availability, and that their most direct influence is on the child's social relations with peers. (Adams & Phillips, 1972; Altus, 1966; Bartlett & Smith, 1966; Bradley & Sanborn, 1969; Breland, 1972; Chittenden *et al.*, 1968; Cicirelli, 1967, 1973a,b; Clausen, 1966; Dandes & Dow, 1969; Hardy, 1972; Otto, 1965; Rhine, 1968; Rosenberg & Sutton-Smith, 1966, 1968, 1969, 1971, 1972; Sampson & Hancock, 1967; Sears, 1961, 1970; Sells & Roff, 1964; Smelser & Stewart, 1968; Stewart, 1967; Weinberg, 1964.)

III

Recurrent Themes

It is difficult to summarize further the research compiled in this review, for the review is itself a summary, and the complexity of the topic requires amplification not further simplification. But it is possible and important to highlight some themes running through the account—themes which are consistently and recurrently revealed by research on the family.

One theme which has not always been fully appreciated in research on the family is that of "bidirectionality" of effects. It has often been assumed that parent-child interaction is essentially a one-way street with parent influencing child. Examination of the mutual effects of parents and children, however, clearly demonstrates the dynamic, reciprocal, transactional nature of human relationships. For example, we now have evidence of the importance of the innate characteristics of the infant for determining both his immediate interpersonal environment and the effect of that environment on his development. As we probe further into family interactions we continue to discover complex causal behavioral sequences; we observe the continuous and progressive interplay between a "plastic" organism and a changeable environment.

One of the most obvious of the infant's innate characteristics is sex, and it is clear that this characteristic is related to parent–child interaction. The onus is on future investigators—even in a "liberated" era—to include this variable in studies of the family. Two further themes of the report are implied in this statement. One is the importance in discussions of caregiving or parental influence of asking the question "for whom?"—boy or girl, active or passive infant, of what age, and so forth. It is impossible to describe or prescribe "good" care without identifying the characteristics of the child. The second theme suggested by the statement is that it is important to build on what we already know in designing, conducting, and interpreting research. Especially in this very complex area, if our knowledge is to be increased it is essential that research build on prior evidence and utilize the most sophisticated methods and techniques available.

Not only the child's sex, but the parent's sex, also, enters significantly into an analysis of parent–child interaction. Evidence suggests that, in our present society, mothers and fathers have different roles in the family and influence their children's development in different ways. In the past, and at present, fathers have been underutilized as caregivers. They may be as ready, willing, and able to participate as mothers, but for the most part they are not as available. The limited research we have on fathers suggests that, with infants, the effects of mother and father are parallel but differ in magnitude as a result of their differential availability to interact with the baby. With preschool children, fathers have been observed to be more strict, demanding, and distant than mothers, and in the school years, to be more likely to provide models of achievement. Currently changing adult roles for men and women may reduce these maternal/paternal differences. Whether they do or not, it is clear that although one-parent families are not necessarily harmful to children's development, in intact families *both* parents influence the achievement and social development of the child. For children to develop optimal patterns of social and intellectual behavior, the same basic qualities of social interaction are valuable in both parents, and it seems that the roles of the parents should be relatively balanced and consistent. However, although consistency and balance between parents is beneficial, this does not imply that parents should necessarily act identically; *variety* among adult caregivers also can enhance development.

One grand theme which emerges is that children's development is related to the care they receive—regardless of who gives it. The research reviewed also suggests some of the significant dimensions of that care. Only in the first three months of the infant's life, it seems, is care for the infant's physical needs the critical aspect of parental caregiving. Children's development of social, emotional and intellectual abilities is greatly influenced by the way their parents behave toward them. Early language development is perhaps most clearly influenced by parental behavior. Even the early babbling of infants is related to adult speech which is directed to the infant and follows his vocalization. For the acquisition of real language—first words and sentences—and for subsequent verbal skill, it is not reinforcement of vocalization but verbal stimulation that is important. The amount, variety, and complexity of speech in face-to-face interaction with an adult clearly influences the child's early language ability. For optimal development of children's language, the adult language model should be responsive to the child's verbal level and cognitive organization and accepting of the child's verbal proposals; speech should be relevant to the child's ongoing activities, responsive to questions, elaborative, and informative. The child's language will develop most efficiently if the complexity of the speech directed to him continues to be only slightly more complex than his current level of skill.

The child's intellectual development is also affected by parents' behavior. Although the time parent and child merely spend together or spend in routine caretaking is not related to the child's competence, stimulating mutual interaction of the pair most certainly is. In general, the more the parent looks, talks, plays, or otherwise interacts with the young child in a stimulating way, the more likely is the child to do well on IQ tests, to explore new places and manipulate new things, to be curious and want to learn about the world, to think the world is interesting and controllable, to be creative, to do well in school—to excel in overall competence. The relation may not be monotonic—that is, beyond some optimal amount of stimulation, more talking, reading, and playing by the parent may be too much, and the child's intellectual development may not be enhanced or may even deteriorate. But no observations in families that have been studied have yet demonstrated such detrimental effects.

Not only is children's development affected by the degree of parental stimulation, but intellectual development is also related to parents' attention and responsiveness to the child's needs, abilities, and expressed desires, and adaptation of the stimulation to the baby's level and interests (changing the mode from physical to verbal and increasing the complexity of stimulation as the child gets older). The teaching strategies and language of the parent of more competent preschool children, for example, are relatively more sophisticated, abstract, and elaborate. Intellectual development is furthered, moreover, not only by parental stimulation but by the parents' acceptance and encouragement of infants' physical exploration—as soon as they become mobile. With older children, too, competence is supported by parental behavior that allows and encourages the child to pursue his own activities with reasonable and rational parental control—control that appeals to reason and feelings rather than imposing rules. In the preschool years children's intellectual progress may be enhanced if the parent pushes a bit—by teaching, reading, playing, talking, and by encouraging independence. Too much pressure for too long a period should not be applied, however. Although children's development at first may be accelerated by demanding, authoritarian parents, that superiority is short-lived, and later, although they perform well in traditional school classes, their scores on tests of intelligence and creativity are low. Providing children with stimulating experiences and a rich environment is an invaluable contribution parents can make to their children's intellectual development. Children need to be left free to explore, manipulate, question, create on their own in that environment. This is true for children of all ages, but seems to be especially important for children in the school years.

This description of the dimensions of parental behavior related to the child's intellectual development raises another theme, which is the multivariate nature of parent-child relations. Children's competence—itself a complex variable—is related not to one or two single, isolated parental behaviors, but to a complex multivariate constellation or pattern of behaviors. The mother who is stimulating also tends to adapt the stimulation to the child's level, to listen as well as to talk, to be responsive and affectionate as well as to exert reasonable control.

In the area of social–emotional behavior, the influence of the child on the parent is most evident. The infant's social expressions—like crying and smiling—have an immediate effect on parents' behavior, and over a longer period of time affect the parents' attachment to the child. Here again, however, the situation is a dynamic transaction, with the parent having a reciprocal impact on the child's behavior. In infancy, there are three social-emotional behaviors which clearly demonstrate this complex relation with parental behavior. The frequency of crying is negatively related to the parents' prompt, consistent response; the amount of eye-to-eye contact between parent and infant is related to the amount of parent-child play; and the frequency of smiling is related to the parent's expression of affection. If the mother is attentive, affectionate, responsive, and plays with the baby often, the child is most likely to develop, before the end of the first year, a pattern of optimal or secure attachment to the mother. The child then is affectionate to the mother, looks at, smiles, talks, and goes to her frequently, misses her when she is gone and greets her on her return, but is able to leave her occasionally to explore other aspects of the environment. The early attachment relation between mother (or other caregiver) and child may be the basis for the child's future relations with other people. If the mother has behaved toward the infant in an affectionate and predictably responsive way, the child will come to expect her—and other people—to respond to his behavior. The child anticipates control and success, enjoyment, and the satisfaction of his needs in new situations and in social interactions with new people. With other family members, strangers, and peers, he initiates social contact, is sensitive to social cues, and is responsive to social advances.

The most mature and competent social behavior of children from three to nine years is independent but friendly, self-confident and assertive, but conforming to group standards when appropriate. Such socially competent children come from families in which parents are attentive and warm. They respect the child's freedom and treat him or her like an independent, relatively mature person. They model positive social behavior and reward both independent achievement and cooperation. They continue to be responsive, helpful, and informative. Discipline is consistent, usually firm, but reasonable and rational; limits are clearly defined, appropriate, and moderate in number; and enforcement is gentle. Children may vary from this optimal balance of assertiveness and friendliness in either direction. Those who are more aggressive usually have parents who are directive, restrictive, hostile, and punitive. These parents model and reward aggressive behavior, and are not consistently responsive to the needs of the child. The behavior of other children is characterized by immature dependency. Their mothers, too, were restrictive, punitive, and nonresponsive to them as infants, but later, in the preschool period, they behave permissively and indulgently and continue to treat the child as an infant.

The development of children in families is also subject to influences other than the behavior of parents. The family milieu is shaped by cultural, social, economic, and geographical factors which affect the behavior of children and parents. It is further affected by the characteristics of *all* the children in the family. Researchers are still struggling to describe critical patterns of parental care—they are even farther from adequately evaluating the influence of these other factors. In this review, an attempt was made to illustrate the potential influence of some of these factors. Socioeconomic status was discussed as a not altogether satisfactory tool for probing the former set of factors; family size and birth order effects for illuminating the latter. From these discussions only a few firm conclusions emerge. One is that the problems associated with lower socioeconomic status generally make occurrence of behavioral patterns described as "optimal" less likely— which is not surprising considering that researchers have been guided by middle-class standards in defining optimal development. Another consistently supported generalization is that first-borns are high achievers and later-borns are more sociable. This generalization tells only a small part of the story, however. The question of sibling effects is complicated by number, age, spacing, and sex of siblings, and by effects both on the child and on the parents. Very few research attempts have been adequate in their examination of these variables.

It is this lack of research that brings us to the final theme revealed, though not stressed, in this review of the literature. That theme addresses the *limitations* of the generalizations we have drawn from research. There are many constraints on the data that were available for this review. In the introduction we mentioned those resulting from methodological problems and inadequate in this area of investigation. Here, we draw attention to another significant kind of limitation—that imposed by cultural context. First, because the review was limited to studies of American families, generalizability is clearly limited to our own society. Further, most studies were of so-called "mainstream" American families—thus restricting generalizability even more to a particular segment of our society. In addition, a more subtle yet perhaps even more important limitation was imposed by the fact that all the data were collected in studies designed and executed by white, middle-class, academic psychologists. This suggests another kind of cultural constraint in our view, a constraint that every researcher should be acutely aware of, though one which they typically ignore. It suggests that although the findings we have just summarized are replicable, recurrent, and apparently robust, they should always be viewed or used with some caution, knowing that we have not examined the full range of possible or existing variation, and knowing that research questions and even results are likely to have been biased by the value orientations of their investigators.

The analysis of child development and family interaction is both exceedingly complicated and immensely important. This review represents one attempt to compile and integrate some of the vast number of isolated studies available in the archives of psychological literature. It reveals that we do know a lot, more now certainly than a decade ago, but it also suggests that we need to go much further in our search for a complete understanding of family dynamics and their impact on child development. And as the roles of adults and children continue to change, as alternative caretaking arrangements become more diverse and more popular, if we are to continue to understand family development, the need for such research will persist.

Part 2

PROPOSITIONS FOR POLICY

IV

Caveats and Cautions

While the United States is still far from being an "experimenting society"—a goal that some have projected for the future—there does seem to be a demand today from planners of public policy for suggestions and solutions based on empirical research. Increasingly, social scientists are being asked to provide information on which to base social policy. In the area of child care, policy makers are asking questions on the effects on children's development of repeated, temporary separations from the mother, on what happens when fathers or other adults act as substitute child-caregivers, on the optimal number of caregivers for any one child, on how many children a caregiver can be expected to care for, on what kinds of care support children's development, on what qualifications, credentials, or regulations are likely to ensure adequate care. These questions reflect issues that are urgent and controversial. Policy makers on all sides want "facts"— facts on which they can build their cases, facts that will help them decide how to spend their dollars, and facts they hope or trust they can obtain from social scientists.

But do social scientists have those "facts"? Not often. There are enormous problems in obtaining answers to policy questions from the data of social science research. Seldom are the answers obvious in the research data. Special efforts, therefore, are necessary to derive policy implications from research. This book represents one such effort to apply empirical data from research on child development in the family to current child-care policy issues. It takes what is perhaps the

most appropriate first step in such a venture—the surveying, compiling, and reviewing of research—a review that weighed, integrated,
and examined data from all investigations of the topic, not just the
most recent or well-known studies—by a nonpartisan and nonpoliti-
cal researcher, and then the derivation from that review of apparently
logical implications or propositions for policy.

The difficulties faced in that process are probably typical of any
similar endeavor. Since they affect the strength and validity of the
policy propositions that follow, they are the subject of this transitional
section of "caveats and cautions." Most of the difficulties encountered
stem from the fact that the psychological research available for review
here was generally not designed with possible policy applications in
mind. The purpose of most of these investigations was to describe
the course of child development rather than to examine how policy
could provide environments to support, enhance, or facilitate development. The particular difficulties referred to are not problems of
research in general, such as those discussed in Part 1, but are specifically problems of deriving policy from research, in particular from the
research reviewed here. Three kinds of problems that constrain the
validity of the policy propositions are a function of the research itself—
those of methodology, incompleteness, and "embeddedness."

Methodology

The research tells us about relationships, not causes and effects. In general,
the results of the psychological studies reviewed here were correlational, and thus did not provide information about the causal direction between children's behavior and features of the environment.
Although studies demonstrated, for example, that children's intellectual competence is related to their mothers' playfulness, they
seldom took measures to discover whether that is because the
mother's play enhances the child's ability, or because the child's
ability leads to the mother's playing more. The consequent difficulty
of going from this kind of correlational evidence to proposing changes
in the environment is obvious.

Research tells us about probabilities, not people. Although the foregoing
methodological problem of cause and effect is one that can be alleviated with improved techniques of statistical analysis and more
appropriate research methods, the problem of probability is an *inevi-*

table aspect of scientific inquiry. Knowledge based on a *sample* of individuals is never certain and absolute. Statistical significance implies only the probability of an event or a behavior's occurrence; generalizations from the data are always limited to identical kinds of subjects under identical kinds of circumstances. Social science evidence, no matter how statistically significant, can never predict a particular case. Moreover, while a variable may appear to make a significant contribution statistically, that contribution may not be socially significant in terms of policy or reality. Criteria of significance for scientists and Congressmen are vastly different, and those engaged in the task of applying research data to policy must be ever mindful not to promote marginal statistical differences with loud cries for changes in policy.

Incompleteness

In addition to these methodological constraints, there were other problems in deriving policy propositions from the research on child development in the family due to important gaps in that research that drastically limit our ability to generalize to the "real world." Some of the gaps—those that are very general, subtle, and constraining—are discussed here; others, more specific, are discussed in the concluding comments to the book.

The research tells us about some people and relationships, but not all. Recruitment and selection of subjects for studies of child development seriously restrict generalization from the results of these investigations. Of course, there is always some problem in generalizing from people who are *willing* to participate as subjects in a study to those who are not—especially as the latter often represent a sizable proportion of the population—but in addition to that unavoidable limitation of subject recruitment, there also often tends to be a deliberate or unconscious bias in the investigator's selection of people who are *invited* to participate. Most frequently, it must be admitted, subjects are recruited for their convenience or for their likelihood to display the kinds of behavior the investigator is interested in. Consequently, the research literature on families places a disproportionate emphasis on white, middle-class families, and relatively neglects families of other social or cultural groups. This is unfortunate, since we know from cross-national and cross-cultural research that culture, race, and ethnicity have an important influence on patterns of intellectual and social competence in children and on patterns of family structure and child rearing; they may even influence relationships between the two kinds of variables. Behavior of children or parents, it is clear, must be interpreted in its socio-cultural context. Children are defined by their culture, and there are few invariant "needs" of childhood that can be stated without references to adult values or preferences. Consequently, the ethnic pluralism and cultural diversity in the United States make tenuous any abstract and grand conclusions about child development even within American society. Ideally, policy propositions would be based on specific research data for different cultural groups. Unfortunately, that specificity is not yet available in the research literature in this area. We do know something about the effects of social class, but almost nothing about the effects of being Greek or Polish or Chicano or middle-class Black in America today. As a result of this significant gap in our knowledge, it was necessary in deriving the following policy propositions to accept the conclusions from the review of research as merely approximations—knowing they apply most closely to white middle-class families and possibly less to other families.

The research tells us how things are, not how they could be. This is another consequence of the fact that the literature reviewed was limited to studies of a single cultural group and to investigations of variation within only that one group. As we have suggested, other patterns or relations in other groups are also possible—patterns that have not yet even been identified by researchers. No comparisons between those relations or patterns and the ones that have been observed in the segment of the population studied in the research reviewed here can be made. Therefore, the patterns that have been judged by researchers in those studies to represent competence are not necessarily optimal (researchers may not yet have observed optimal) or, in fact, necessarily "competent" in any culture other than the one in which they were observed. From a review of research on a single culture or cultural group we cannot draw any universal conclusions or make any comparative evaluations. Ultimately, it may be the case that there are some rights and wrongs of caregiving independent of cultural memberships and values, but we cannot conclude so at this point from the research reviewed here. Again, our conclusions from the research must be viewed as only "here and now" approximations, and the propositions that follow from those approximations as culture-specific and culture-relative.

Research tells us how things were, not how they will be. Another form that incompleteness in social science research takes is that of obsolescence. If we are to make propositions for policy that are appropriate for current conditions in the world, there is a continuing need to monitor secular changes. But psychological researchers can never really quite keep up with rapid changes in technology, social movement, or economic situations—or with their resultant impacts on children's environments. This once again points to the need to regard empirical conclusions as approximations—time-bound as well as culture-bound.

Research tells us how things are, not how they should be. The final form of incompleteness in the research reviewed here that presented problems for deriving policy propositions was that research is descriptive, not normative. Research offers no explicit guidance to the policy planner or proposer about what behaviors are desirable or good. That is only appropriate. Scientific writing should be as free of personal prejudices and values as it is possible to be. But it is obvious, then, that policy decisions cannot be based solely on scientific research evidence or any other "facts." In the end, policy and policy propositions must rest on the ethics, values, personal experience, and accumulated wisdom of the policy maker or proposer.

Embeddedness

Research may not tell us how things really are. Although, as we have just suggested, scientific literature tends to be appropriately free of *explicit* value judgments and normative statements, there are inevitable value orientations *implicit* in the research. Such is the result of the "embeddedness" of research in the ideology and value system of the researcher and of the predominant society. As we have already pointed out, such values affect *who* the researcher studies; they also affect *what* is studied, *why* it is studied, and *how* it is studied. In general, it must be said that although there may be consensus among research findings—and that is encouraging—generalizations from those findings are really only about the *literature*, not about the *real world*. To draw policy ideas from such generalizations, it is necessary to act *as if* the research were authentic, accurate, generalizable, and representative of real life—but some skepticism and tentativeness should always accompany propositions based on evidence which is so clearly biased and limited.

In addition to these difficulties or limitations that were a function of the research reviewed, there are several further sources of concern or caution implicit in the policy propositions made in this book. First, there is the embeddedness of the propositions in the ideology and values of the person who derived them. Clearly, as we have suggested, this is unavoidable since in order to explore policy implications, generalization and inference beyond the data are necessary. It is, however, a bias that the reader should be aware of. In this particular case, the filter through which the policy propositions were drawn was, perhaps unfortunately, not unlike that of much of the research that was reviewed—it being the value system of an academic, psychological researcher (also young, female, middle-class, WASP, and Canadian). Originally it was hoped in presenting the policy propositions, at least, to keep the research "facts" distinct from interpretation, implication, and speculation. In practice, that turned out to be impossible; and in the discussion that follows the two are inextricably linked. Although they always started from what research evidence suggests may be "fact," the propositions and policy suggestions are, in large measure, a personal invention, representing just one of many possible perspectives, and they should be viewed as such and accepted only with caution.

A second concern is the even deeper embeddedness of every adult and child in American society. The economic and caste structure of society has unexplored yet perhaps overriding importance in children's lives, experiences, and development. Here we have focused on the interpersonal level of that experience, but the underlying determination of children's or parents' behavior that is imposed by the structural context of society must be pointed out as a reason for caution in making and interpreting propositions for public policy. Children, parents, researchers, and policy-makers are all embedded in the fabric of American society and reflect and are constrained by its structure.

Finally, *after* policy implications of research have been explored and propositions suggested as they are in the following pages, there remain the concerns of practicability and implementation, of trying to make the propositions fit with the realities of present-day America, and, further of trying to predict the long-range effects of such policies if enacted. The implication could be drawn from the literature reviewed here, for example, that the "best" kind of family to care for children would have two parents and two children (a boy and a girl), live in a safe neighborhood, have enough money for its physical needs, and then some more for books, toys, and travel. Such an implication does not seem particularly useful for guiding policy or practice, however. As we have suggested, the standards drawn from the research available are probably not "best" for all families or for every family; but also, to confront the issue of implementation, even if it were worthwhile, this goal is unlikely to be achievable. About the problems of implementing the propositions made here or about their possible solutions, little is said in this book. The propositions were not scrutinized in the harsh light of everyday reality, nor were they tested against the standard of current child-care policies—for our concern here was not with practicality or feasibility. I hope the propositions and suggestions made are more usable than that particular example, but they are, still, "idealistic." In real life, undoubtedly, it would not be possible to implement all, or maybe any, of them—but that is not their purpose. It is hoped, rather, that the propositions suggested here will serve to clarify some of the issues and provide grounds for choice when policy compromises are, as they inevitably will be, necessary, and that they will assist policy makers in assigning priorities to policies affecting the care and environments of young children. If we are to improve the quality of life for children in this country, we need to examine the *possibilities* of such proposals.

In addition to confessing to the idealism of these propositions, I also wish to make it clear that I make no claims for their originality or for their completeness. They represent only the implications of one particular, and limited, body of literature for some, also limited, policy issues of interest and concern. Propositions about day care, for example, do not include all that could or should be said about day-care policy, but only statements that most clearly found support in the reviewed research on families. Sometimes the research results reviewed here offered support for policies that already exist; sometimes they suggested new kinds of programs or policies. I have made no effort to separate these suggestions on the basis of their current status in United States policy, nor have I tried to include the research implications for all extant policies concerning children. If particular kinds of policy are not discussed, it does not mean they are less acceptable than those suggested, but only that the research reviewed did not strike me as relevant to them. Some readers will undoubtedly be dissatisfied to find no direct link to or evaluation of current programs and policies. That, however, was not my purpose nor my assignment. My task was to present some ideas derived from research, free from the constraints of current legalities, limitations, and legislation. The propositions described in the next chapter are just that— propositions—which are to be discussed, debated, and deliberated; not prescribed, programmed, or pushed.

V

Propositions

Fifteen propositions for child-care policy, derived from the preceding review and interpretation of research on child development in families, and limited by the restrictions described in the preceding chapter, are stated and discussed in this section. They address "policy" at various levels and contain suggestions that may be helpful to state or federal legislators, city officials, hospital and social-service administrators, directors of day-care and educational programs for young children, and individual parents or other adults concerned with child care, child welfare, or child development. As we have suggested in the previous chapter, they are not intended to be specific recommendations for policies but are offered as guidelines for deliberation about policy at any of these levels. Each is stated simply and positively, but their form, it must be understood, is to be considered that of a proposition not an authoritarian pronouncement. The implicit preface or prefix for each proposition is "The research reviewed suggests that..." or "On the basis of the research reviewed, it is proposed that...." This must be borne in mind throughout.

These propositions are organized into five broad categories: the importance of variety in policies, components of child care, the family as a child-caring environment, alternative child-care environments, and accessibility and authority of policy. As the result of this organization there is some overlap between propositions and some redundancy in discussions of the implications of research for each proposal. This is the inevitable result of applying the same research literature within each of several individual policy categories. Another problem that arises from this division into categories is the danger that particular propositions or categories of propositions will be taken individually out of context. Despite their division, it is important to consider all the propositions *together*. Individual propositions about specific child-care issues such as divorce, adoption, day care, or parent education should be considered as *options* within the *variety* of programs and policies that Proposition 1 suggests should be made available, and these options, as Proposition 15 makes clear, are to be selected by *individual* families, not imposed by "the State." Our aim in all these propositions, it must be stressed, is to suggest opportunities that are likely to benefit children, not to propose policies or programs that would force families into a single "ideal-family" mold.

The Importance of Variety

1. *Policies on child care should show variety that respects and accommodates differences in age, need, and cultural values*

One generalization that stands out in the research on child care and development is that people are different—girls from boys, fathers from mothers, rich from poor, infants from young children. Differences between individuals create a range of needs, goals, behaviors, roles, relations. Clearly, we need to support many different solutions and arrangements, programs and models, in order to provide individual choice among a variety of options, and to provide the most appropriate care or service for each person. Any policy should be complex, therefore, not a simple, single recommendation. We know that the infant's constitutional predispositions determine to some extent what kind of environment will most readily enhance development. We know that children develop better in environments or with caregivers that "match" their needs and abilities. One can assume that the same is true for adults. Consequently, a *variety* of programs is called for to meet the needs of different families and different children, in different circumstances, with different cultural values.

AGE.   Specifically, we would propose that different services be provided for children of different *ages*. Judging from past experience, there is some danger that a program which has been successful with one age group will be imposed on older or younger children without adequate examination of the feasibility or sensibility of such a plan. A case that comes to mind is the nursery school or kindergarten curriculum lifted with little alteration from first grade, which contains many activities inappropriate for three- and four-year-olds. Children clearly have different needs and abilities as they grow older—and these differences sometimes have profound implications for the content of educational or child-care programs. In fact, one of the central qualities of "good" parenting is that the care or stimulation offered is appropriate for the child's developmental level. An example from the family literature is that while a lot of physical contact with mother is beneficial for the young infant, at a later age too much physical contact with the caregiver may be detrimental. Or, to give another example, although a lot of "social" stimulation from the parents in the first few years of life seems to facilitate children's development, as children get older specific verbal content of the stimulation increases in importance. One final example concerns 4- or 5- or 6-year-old children who are usually quite independent enough to be in a group program; earlier than that, however, separation from mother may be somewhat stressful and therefore would call for selection of caregivers who are especially warm and nurturant.

This need for *age*-differentiated programs or services, illustrated by the literature on child development in the family, may be obvious to parents and child development professionals, but it may not be so clear to legislators or policy-makers. Their first question is not always "How old are the children you are proposing this bill for?" Some political spokesmen have even suggested that a reason for supporting early childhood education programs is that this will allow children to complete their education sooner—as if assuming that you can just push the elementary and secondary school curriculum down a few years and get kids through it by the time they are 12 or 13. Whether or not earlier graduation is indeed desirable is a perfectly legitimate and important question that we might be concerned with—but it is a question quite apart from the issue of whether to start formal schooling at age 3. Any programmatic policies for child care would be improved if they were age-specific and age-appropriate.

Another hope expressed by policy makers is that putting children from poor homes in good institutional day-care centers when they are young will decrease the incidence of later juvenile delinquency. Research evidence does support the statement that very early care is critical to children's later development, because it affects all subsequent interaction of the child with his or her environment—even if the child is later put into a completely different environment. This does *not* imply that good care or an enriched environment in early life will "inoculate" the child permanently against later bad or inadequate environments; development and behavior are always affected by the *current*, ongoing environment as well as the earlier one. (Intellectual gains resulting from experience in preschool programs, for example, are only maintained in school situations which support further development.) However, the relationship between early care and later behavior does suggest that if the early environment does not allow for the development of certain skills and cognitive structures, the loss may never be fully recovered by later remediation. It may not be impossible to make up for lost time—but it is unlikely. Moreover, the cost (in time or dollars) of later intervention, whether or not it is effective, is likely to exceed the cost of early preventive measures because of the stabilization of the environment and parent-child interaction that occurs over time. Clearly, there is need for *both early* and *continuing* education and care.

NEED.   We would also propose that child-care policies meet the diversity of needs of American families—needs related to family size, family income, parental work status and employment opportunity, parents' educational needs and desires, and arrangements for child care open to and needed by the family. To satisfy all such needs, it follows that child-care policies should be comprehensive and heterogeneous. They might include, for example, support for cooperative group child care *and* for improved family care—economic *and* educational, crisis *and* continuous; relief from financial pressure for poor parents *and* relief from full-time child care for affluent parents; flexibility in work schedules for mothers (maternity leaves, part-time work, job sharing, sabbaticals, school holidays off, etc.) *and* the same for fathers.

The needs of one group of families in particular stand out, and because of their special significance are given special mention and examination here. Those are the needs of the so-called "disadvantaged," "poor," or "lower class" families. These families have frequently been the targets of social science research, most commonly in studies contrasting them with the more affluent "middle-class" families. Such studies have typically found differences in patterns of child care and sometimes child behavior associated with socioeconomic status. Some of these were reviewed earlier. Unfortunately, from these studies there is no way to separate the relative effects of the components of SES—occupation, education, and income. Consequently, solely economic or solely educational policy proposals are simply not inferable. It is not valid to refer to low SES families as merely "poor" and therefore propose income redistribution or a minimum guaranteed income to change their behavior. Nor is it any more accurate to call them merely "uneducated" and propose educational solutions for all their problems. At this point in time, therefore, solutions at both levels would seem to be advisable (and may turn out to be necessary). Intervention should offer *both* educational and economic opportunities for parents, even within this restricted range of the population.

Studies have often compounded the difficulty of ascertaining the reasons for observed SES differences, moreover, by not employing adequate controls for religion, race, geographical location, or ethnic group. We cannot say, therefore, whether behaviors associated with lower socioeconomic status are the result of poverty, ignorance, a different culture, social pressure or prejudice, genetic potential, or all of these. Once again, the advisability of a range of policy efforts is obvious.

In addition, it should be noted that patterns of child care or child performance associated with a particular social-class level are not *inevitably* observed in families from that social stratum; the variability within class is great, and the overlap between classes is significant. Programs directed at behavior change should certainly not be restricted to parents of lower socioeconomic status, as there has been some tendency in "compensatory education" and other categorical social programs. In fact, the patterns of child care more often observed in lower SES families are sometimes more supportive of child development than those observed in middle-class families. For the first six months of life, for example, infants in less affluent families are apt to receive more attention than those in middle-class homes. Intervention for poor children at this age should probably be physical—nutritional, hygienic, or economic—rather than educational (particularly as these infants are more likely to be born "at risk" physically). During the period of infancy the only behavioral difference among mothers reported in the child development literature to be related to SES is that some mothers talk more deliberately and distinctively to their infants. The less verbally stimulating and responsive behavior of other mothers may be due to the belief that one does not need to talk to babies who obviously do not understand and cannot talk back. They may not appreciate that children need to hear language models in order to learn to speak and understand language. If this is true, it would seem that this misperception could be easily corrected. A TV or newspaper campaign—directed at all adults who care for children—might be undertaken, which would suggest that one important way adults can help young children develop their abilities is by talking to them—even before they know how to talk. It might also be pointed out that when children are able to express themselves in words they do not need to cry, stamp, point, or grunt as often. Some hints could be included about how and when to talk to children—in short, simple sentences about what is going on, using interesting and specific words, when the child is "listening," after the child has vocalized, and when the mother is giving him her full attention.

By the time the infant is about six months old, although mothers and children of all socioeconomic levels still spend the same amount of time together, and although the infants still behave similarly, some mothers, typically those of higher income and education groups, have been observed to interact with the children more frequently and more actively, especially verbally, and to be more stimulating, playful, and affectionate, and less restrictive and punitive. There are a number of possible reasons for these differences. Those mothers observed to interact less with their children may have become so burdened by other household, economic, or emotional pressures that such interaction is not possible. They may find it easier to care for helpless infants than active, impudent children. They may have become bored with being at home or taking care of children. They may be unaware of the potential benefits for children of stimulating interaction with an adult, or they may not enjoy such activities. If the latter reasons are valid, then an educational program for these mothers, focusing on the joy and value of actively interacting with and caring for young children, would be promising.

Because of the important cognitive, social, and language changes that occur in the second half of a child's first year, the ideal target time for such educational programs for parents would seem to be from the time the child is six months old until about two years. If the principles of effective child care were incorporated by mothers at this point in the child's development, it might then be possible for them to phase out of the educational program so that only periodic contacts with a child-development counselor or relatively brief "refresher" or "reinterpretation" sessions would be necessary.

CULTURAL VALUES.   A third dimension of difference that should be considered in planning policy for families in the United States is that of culture, race, or ethnicity. As we pointed out earlier, there are differences in parents' values and attitudes toward child care that are related to their membership in a cultural or subcultural group—differences that unfortunately are not yet clearly articulated in the research literature on child development. Although there are undoubtedly many basic human needs held in common by all parents living and raising children in the United States, policies should be formulated to account for stylistic and attitudinal differences that reflect cultural identities. This is not to suggest that specific programs or interventions be targeted to particular ethnic groups—that all Afro-American mothers be assigned to model "A," while all Greek-American mothers enroll in program "B"—not at all. It does suggest that sufficient variety be incorporated within any policy to allow parents to choose the particular program or arrangement or benefit that is most compatible with their values for children's behavior, methods of discipline, academic learning, interpersonal style, roles of mother, father, grandmother, etc.

In general, in making the point that policies should be responsive to individual differences, there is some danger that this will be interpreted as suggesting that what *is, will be* or *ought to be.* That is *not* the intention of the proposition. On the contrary, as the following propositions make clear, change can and should be effected—but within the context of responding to individual differences. There is a range of expression for acceptable and competent behavior of parents and children, and it only makes sense to offer programs to match individual differences in the way people *are*—in order to let them move more effectively toward what they can *become.*

There is also a danger that recommending a variety of programs will be interpreted as opposing a national policy for children. Again, this is not the intention of the proposition. Although at the local level a range of different programs and types of program should be available to meet the needs of different children and families, there is undoubtedly also a need for unified coordination of all these programs at the national level. A comprehensive and complex national policy for children and youth could provide such coordination and establish reasonable priorities among programs affecting young people.

2. We should foster environments and programs that promote the basic competence of all young children, and competence should be defined to include emotional and social qualities as well as intellectual-cognitive skills

Central and foremost in efforts to devise policies that will affect the care of children should be the examination of goals—goals of the policies and goals for children that are implied by the policies. Too often, it seems, this step is omitted from policy deliberation. Too often it is considered more urgent and feasible to discuss the relative *costs* of different policies—in terms of taxpayers' dollars, not psychological effects—rather than the kind of children or adults we are creating and the kind we want. As a nation and as individuals, we would be well advised to examine and articulate our goals for child development and then to examine how various policies effect these goals. All policies have goals—implicit or explicit; if they are made explicit, they can serve as reasonable bases for policy decisions.

Goals for child development held by individuals and ideas about the kinds of children we want, are, it must be noted, both personal and culture-specific. Within our own society, there are apparent differences in child-rearing goals of different segments or subcultures in the American population, for example, differences in what "intelligence" is, differences in the value placed on competition versus cooperation, in the emphasis on female assertiveness, or on children's independence, aggression, or obedience. These differences take on added significance as our "melting pot" rhetoric is challenged by a philosophy of ethnic pluralism. Moreover, such differences in child-rearing goals are not inappropriate or merely whimsical. Usually the goals expressed are best suited for real-life conditions faced by children in different subcultural environments. For any particular child, it is obvious, the most valuable skills or characteristics are determined by the environment he or she is in or is to enter. Clearly, diversity of goals is present in our society, and warranted.

However, significant consensus on many, probably most, child-rearing goals also exists; differences are usually shadings of emphasis rather than complete opposites. The following set of goals is the one on which the policy propositions in this book are based. They represent the author's view, but also they are proposed here as goals likely to be embraced by the majority of parents in the United States and as goals that are legitimate and desirable for policy aims.

The first goal we might adopt for guiding child-care policies is to avoid harm and to provide for the *physical survival* of all children. This is a minimum requirement and of highest priority. But clearly it is not sufficient for enlightened policy. A second general goal for policy that goes beyond this minimum is to try to offer children a *pleasant childhood*—a childhood free from hunger and pain, abuse and neglect, pressure and stress, insecurity and fear; a time for children to be themselves, find themselves, and express themselves. This is a goal that has seldom found explicit expression in policy. Perhaps it is too obvious, too difficult to define, too "unscientific," or does not sound important enough. I believe, however, it is an important goal, and one that does not need scientific or economic justification. As a nation, in setting policy for children, we tend to be overly concerned with "long-range outcomes" of our programs. We do not consider it a sufficient reason to institute a program that would make children happier; we also want proof that it will make them smarter or better when they are older. The point of expressing this goal of a "pleasant childhood" is to suggest that we treat childhood as an important period for its own sake, not only because "the child is father to the man. . . ." Adult life, as we all know too well, is fraught with pain and pressure; if children can be protected from these stresses for a time, that itself should be a significant, if not sufficient, reason to justify some policies.

The third general goal proposed is to promote *development* of children—development in both physical and psychological spheres of activity. For our purposes, the goal of physical development includes not just good health but physical vitality and motor skill. Psychological development is more complex; it comprises a wide range of skills, behaviors, and qualities. Intellectual ability is the aspect of psychological development that has been most popular as the focus of policies for young children. Nearly all our educational efforts, including the attempts at compensatory education begun in the mid-1960's, have taken as their major goal the enhancement of intellectual development. Unfortunately, the designers and sponsors of those programs have been almost exclusively interested in a narrow range of intellectual skills—those reflected in tests of IQ, academic knowledge, and school achievement. While these skills are valuable, we would suggest that strict emphasis on academic or cognitive training—to the exclusion of other goals—is misplaced. There are many important aspects of development not touched by such training: in the development of thought (the development of attention, persistence, curiosity, exploration, problem-solving, anticipation of consequences, and perspective-taking, to mention a few); in the development of resourcefulness and coping strategies; in the development of language and communication; and in the development of social relations and emotional strengths. These latter socio-emotional aspects of development are worthy of much increased emphasis, for they are fragile qualities, and yet essential for a satisfying life in our fragmented and mobile society. The goal we would propose here is to give priority to developing in children the capacity for caring and sharing—for developing trust, emotional attachment, sympathy, cooperation, warmth and affection, expression of deep feelings, willingness to help others, and a commitment to other people. In addition to these social qualities, we would also desire for children an inner sense of identity, personal wholeness, self-worth, and confidence—a balance between social and selfish qualities.

Our goal for the development of children might thus be summarized as promoting the development of the "whole child" or developing children's general "overall competence." This concept of competence is one that emerges from the literature on child development in the family. In this use of the term, competence is reflected in *all* the child's behavior—intellectual test performance, exploration of the physical environment, knowledge of social situations, relations with other people, use and understanding of language, and involvement in creative pursuits. Most often, in the early years, children are judged to be competent in a *variety* of areas. It is not merely that competent children learn to talk sooner or score higher on IQ tests, although these qualities are included, but they also are friendly and cooperative, independent and assertive, sensitive and articulate. The notion of a general overall competence, then, provides a reasonable goal that should be sought for all children; such competence provides a basis for further development.

Within that overall goal or quality, however, there is room for individual variation. Specific patterns or expressions of competence depend on personal, temperamental, and cultural variation. The balance between prosocial behavior (cooperation, altruism) and self-aggrandizing behavior (competition, achievement), for example, may be tilted slightly one way or the other in competent individuals. Some individuals may express their competence in a single speciality—like art or athletics—others demonstrate it "all round." There are many ways of expressing competence; we should avoid a single standard rating system such as IQ. With the proviso of first promoting children's basic overall competence—intellectual and socio-emotional—we would support diversity, variation, and expansion of possibilities for development.

Components of Care

Even though children themselves have a strong impact on their caregivers, and even though development is ultimately limited by biological and genetic factors—the clear consensus that emerges from the review of research on child development and family interaction is that the child's psychological development is profoundly and significantly influenced by the kind of care he or she receives. Unfortunately, it is not possible to specify "ideal" care without knowing the individual child, caregiver, and circumstances. One cannot recommend particular caretaking practices without taking into account the infant's natural temperament, persistence, rhythm, tendency to approach or avoid, attention span—characteristics which must be adapted to by the caregiver. Nor is it possible to define "optimal" care except in the context of the caregiver's personal goals and cultural values. Within these constraints, however, and following from the goals articulated in the previous section, some general propositions on beneficial caregiving qualities can be formulated. Such propositions follow.

3. *Adult caregiving should provide children with appropriate stimulation, variety, acceptance, responsiveness, and affection*

It is possible, first, to describe in general terms the kinds of care that are most beneficial to children of different ages. In the first three months, care for physical needs (food, warmth, hygiene) is central. After that early period, infants thrive when caregivers interact with them frequently, regularly, affectionately, physically, and playfully;

care adequately for nutritional and other physical needs; and are responsive to the infant's needs and expressive behavior. With
toddlers, it is beneficial if caregivers, as well as interacting frequently
and responsively, are verbally stimulating, place few restrictions on
the child's activities allowing him or her to explore independently,
and provide the child with some pleasant experiences with other
adults. As children grow older they develop most adequately when
caregivers continue to behave warmly and attentively; accept exploration and expression; set limits and use control which is reasonable
and rational; use teaching and language strategies which are elaborative; stimulate intellectual growth by reading, talking, teaching, playing with toys, and providing a novel variety of toys; and encourage
the child's independence.

It is also possible to extract from the literature reviewed information
on relations between specific aspects of children's development and
particular components of care. Language development seems to be
accelerated and facilitated by frequent verbal stimulation by an adult
in one-to-one interaction with the child, when the adult's speech is
varied, relevant to the child's activity, and appropriately complex
(just slightly more than the child's speech). Cognitive development is
enhanced by the caregiver's frequent looking, talking, playing, and
later teaching and reading—as this stimulation is adapted and responsive to the child's needs, abilities, and expressed desires. Social
development depends first on frequent affectionate and responsive
interaction with primary caregivers, and, later, on opportunities for
interaction with peers and other people. Social competence which
balances friendliness with assertiveness, conformity with independence, is related to discipline that is respectful and rational.

In sum, speaking of necessity very generally, for the development
of overall competence in children—the kind of competence proposed
as a valuable goal for our child care policies—the qualities of adult
care that seem to be important are *stimulation* (from things and
people), *appropriateness* (level and schedule adapted to the individual
child), *variety* (in language, people, toys), *acceptance* (reasonable
limits, firmly but gently enforced), *responsiveness* (prompt, consistent,
elaborative responses to the child's behaviors), and *affection* (expressed verbally, facially, physically). As the child gets older, it seems
that adult behavior should increase in level of complexity, scope of
responsiveness, and span of interactive and affective distance. Also,
the amount of freedom, privacy, and independence the adult allows

the child to explore his or her own interests should be increased. It is these kinds of behavior that seem important for children's well-being and development rather than time spent by the parent in caretaking or the use of particular caretaking routines.

Later propositions will bear on policies for supporting and promoting these desirable kinds of care. For example, although these conclusions or generalizations are based on observations of parents, it is not unlikely that the same qualities are appropriate for other caregivers in the child's world—teachers, babysitters, and siblings. Therefore, such qualities of caregiving might well be stressed in any training or educational programs for parents or caregivers. Moreover, they could be used as guidelines in selecting and preparing persons to care for children (foster or adoptive parents, babysitters, day-care personnel). It is less useful to focus efforts on finding people who are skilled at feeding or diapering, who can pass tests and courses, can read and write, who are ethnically identical to the children, who have worked with children for many years—although all these may help—except as these characteristics are related to the *behavioral* qualities described above. An implication that follows for procedures of training and selecting child-care workers is that such procedures involve opportunities to observe the person interacting with real live children (preferably the same children for whom the person will be caring). Since it is not likely that these desirable qualities can be learned from books, new instructional procedures, which would include increased practical experience, seem necessary.

4. *Quantity of child care (number of hours, number of adult caregivers per child) is not to be equated with quality of care*

These two words—quantity and quality—when applied to child care have sometimes led to unnecessary confusions and misleading contrasts. It seems worthwhile to examine some of these confusions here. The amount of time an adult caregiver spends with a child, interacting with him or her, or actively caring for his or her physical needs is usually referred to as the "quantity" of care. "Quality" of care refers to the particular *kind* and *mode* of behavior involved in the interaction. In particular, as used by current researchers, quality refers to the stimulating, playful, responsive, affectionate nature of the care, the style and content of language and teaching, the method of discipline, and the variety and appropriateness of behavior.

One confusion between quantity and quality has arisen out of the common practice in day-care parlance to equate "quality child care" with a high adult-child ratio. This is understandable, since a concrete and legislatible index of "quality" was necessary. But, in point of fact, the adult-child ratio is an index of probable *quantity* of adult contact not *quality* of care. Even with a ratio of one adult to one child what matters is that the adult like, understand, and care about and for the child.

A second confusion has come from a misinterpretation of a research-based generalization. It is patently obvious that some minimal quantity of care is necessary for children's survival. And, in fact, the amount of parental care—in the sense of active interaction not merely the time spent in the same room as the child—has been shown by research to be positively related to children's development. However, it has also been observed in research that sheer quantity of care *alone* does not ensure optimal or even adequate development. This latter empirical finding has sometimes led to the assertion that the *quality* of care is more important than the *quantity*. While this generalization is statistically valid, it can easily be misinterpreted. If taken to its extreme, the statement can lead to the inference that if a child gets 10 minutes of "quality" care every day, it does not matter if he or she is left alone or in a poor environment for the rest of the day. This is obviously false! In the first place, it is difficult to separate the two in practice—not only because "quality" assumes *some* "quantity," but because mothers who behave in a "qualitatively superior" way also tend to spend more time with their children in active interaction. In the second place, we do not have explicit evidence about what happens to children who are regularly exposed to different caregiving environments which *differ* markedly in "quality." It seems reasonable to expect that what matters is *overall* quality (i.e., over the whole 24-hour day), perhaps in proportion to the amount of time the child spends in each setting (i.e., the relative quantity of quality). Quantity is a necessary though not sufficient condition for child care. A short amount of good "quality" care does not obviate the need for substantial "quantity" of care.

5. *Policy should promote continuity of child care*

The issue of continuity comes up repeatedly in discussions about the care of children. Research on the family confirms the importance of the concern by suggesting that indeed the continuity of care—the balance and consistency between parents, and the consistency, pre-dictability or stability of parental behavior over time—is important to children's development. Children benefit from learning that they have some control over the environment and that they can anticipate events; they thrive on a strong emotional attachment to some other person or persons; parents need to learn to respond accurately and consistently to their children's expressions and demands. These processes, for both parents and children, suggest the value of con-tinuous, continuing, regular contact between parent and child. By extrapolation, one would expect this to apply to nonparental caregiv-ers as well (adoptive or foster parents, sitters, or day-care persons).

We have little information about the effects of lack of consistency between parents and concurrent nonparental caregivers, for example, between a parent and a day-care teacher, but it seems sensible to expect that although it may not be as critical as intrapersonal consis-tency, some degree of consistency here would make the world easier for the child to understand. The adults' behavior and attitudes need not be identical, since some variety enhances development, but what should be avoided is marked and overt conflict between the two caregivers or complete disruption or contradiction of the child's pre-vious experiences. One implication that follows is that it is important for parents and other caregivers to communicate with each other on their values and behavior toward children. Thus the need for consis-tency of care provides one justification for parent participation in day-care or early education programs.

We know somewhat more about the dangers of *temporal* inconsis-tency of care and caregiving environments (e.g., children who experi-ence numerous shifts from foster home to foster home). The det-rimental effect on development of such temporal discontinuity also has implications for day-care policy. It clearly suggests the need for stable employees in day care (whether center or home). This in turn suggests the need for some reward system to make staying in the day-care setting attractive (status, salary, educational options, career ladder promotions, etc.) and for hiring practices which select adults who like working with children and are likely to remain. A further suggestion would be that children stay in the same setting or class for a substantial period of time—which in turn leads to endorsement of heterogeneous age grouping in early childhood programs.

Children's need for stability and continuity is one reason that the family has provided an optimal environment for raising children—

since a family ideally constitutes a life-long network of committed and concerned relatives. The current trend (cf. Bronfenbrenner, 1975) toward more frequent divorce and remarriage may endanger the stability of child care which families can provide by leading to temporal discontinuity of parenting and possibly to inconsistency between successive stepparents. From this perspective, it makes sense to recommend counseling services for families in marital conflict in order to prevent unnecessary divorce. When divorce is necessary, a custody decision to place the child with one committed parent (either mother or father) who would provide needed stability for the child, with some continued contact with the other parent, might be preferred to splitting the child's time equally between the two parents. Again, the individual case would have to be determined by the parents' attitudes toward divorce, the child, and child care, and by the child's feelings for and about the parents, but in any procedures for the disposition of children, stability, continuity, and consistency of care should be a central concern.

6. Children need a stimulating physical environment, but variety and quality of materials are more important than quantity, and adult participation in play is more important than the materials themselves

While it is clear that a barren, nonstimulating environment is detrimental to infants' perceptual and cognitive development, that a child with *no* toys or books to play with will suffer, it does not follow that we should support the expenditure of vast sums for elaborate toys and materials for children. Research suggests that over a certain minimal number, the sheer quantity of toys does not enhance development as much as does the variety, complexity, and responsiveness of the objects available. A fairly small number of toys may be adequate if they are of different kinds and are regularly added to or replaced. While fancy and expensive mobiles have been observed to accelerate perceptual-cognitive development of infants in institutions, they are in fact not necessary for infants in typical homes. The opportunity to watch the movement of family members is stimulating and interesting to the infant. A variety of small household objects that the infant or child can manipulate freely and has some control over is adequate for early development. Opportunity for the child to explore whatever is in the physical environment is also beneficial. But the most beneficial kind of play object of all for the young child is one provided by the mother or other caregiver—one she shows, gives, demonstrates, or plays with, one that is at an appropriate level of complexity for the child's ability. A model of supportive services for families might, with some justification, include a toy library or a toy exchange—but *people* are necessary mediators and adapters of the child's physical environment. Advice to parents or demonstration by the toy librarian, or some general courses in what children like to play with and how adults can participate in play with children, might be offered—at the library, in school, at a pediatric clinic, at the super-market, or on television.

Television is another component of the physical environment for almost all children in the United States—a component that arouses controversy and concern in caregivers and citizens. For its advocates, TV is the hope of the future—the way to give all children equal oppor-tunities for learning; to its opponents, television represents a poten-tial threat to children's minds and care. Both positions find some support in the results of research on the effects of television viewing on children's behavior and development (cf. review of this research by Stein & Friedrich, 1975).

The pessimists find support in research showing that young chil-dren who spend more time watching TV often lag behind their peers developmentally (Carew, 1975). Yet this research does not prove that the lag is the direct result of television viewing *per se*; more likely, the lag follows from the more limited interaction of these children with live persons who behave in stimulating and responsive ways. Well-documented negative effects of watching specific TV content—notably, violence—also give credence to fears about TV. Children who watch violent programs—and it might be mentioned that car-toons are highest in violent content of any kind of program currently on TV—subsequently act more aggressively and are less cooperative and helpful, are less willing to delay gratification and to share, are less likely to exert self-control, and are more anxious and fearful. On the other hand, the impact of specific TV content on children's be-havior can also give comfort to those who consider television helpful or hopeful for social reform. For just as violent programs lead to "negative" outcomes, "positive" programs lead to "positive" out-comes. Specifically, programs with high prosocial content—like "Mr. Rogers' Neighborhood"—with repeated viewing, are likely to in-crease children's cooperation, sharing, and helping; cognitively stimulating programs—like "Sesame Street" or "The Electric Company"—lead to intellectual gains in their viewers.

Television, for good or evil, is a potent part of every child's experience. Adults can and should, therefore, be taught to utilize TV as an educational and socializing resource. To do so, they need:

1. Information on the potential effects of television and of specific types of television programs on children's behavior and development—such as that we have just described.

2. A guide to the content of current programs. The networks' announcements that certain programs "may not be suitable for younger viewers" is one small step in this direction; there are also books available offering information on program content. These efforts should be supported and extended—as should efforts to increase the amount and quality of programming appropriate for children.

3. Guidance concerning their own role vis-à-vis children's viewing and the effects of TV. The role of adults with television, interestingly, seems to parallel their role with toys. There is little doubt that the television-viewing habits of parents influence those of their children (cf. Stein & Friedrich, 1975). Parents serve as models, and children, on their own, select programs of the same type viewed by their parents. Adult approval or disapproval of program content, expressed verbally, however, has little effect on whether children *imitate* what they see on TV. (In one study of 5- to 8-year-olds, adult reactions to televised violence affected children's behavior only while the adult was still present.) What adults *do*, once again, carries more weight with children than what they *say*. It has also been observed that when the parent watches programs with prosocial or cognitive content *with* the child, this has a strong influence on the child's absorption of that content. This effect may occur because parents learn from the program what is appropriate to teach children and thus are similarly stimulating in their other interactions with the child; or, it may occur because the parent mediates the television program for the child in the same way as he or she mediates the rest of the material environment—thus making television viewing, like play with toys, more stimulating, less passive, and more understandable for the child. Research has not yet established the reason for the observed relation, but it is clear that children's development may be enhanced via this medium, too, when it is shared with the caregiver. Finally,

the role of the adult can include provision of play materials to augment the impact of television content. "Props"—like Sesame Street books or muppets or Batman capes—can lead to children's more active participation during the program and to "rehearsal" or incorporation of program content in play between viewings. Such materials can be used by parents or other caregivers deliberately and with forethought to enhance the program content they value. These are suggestions and facts about television that adults should be acquainted with—perhaps, in fact, they can be communicated effectively via the same medium.

The Family as a Child-Care Environment

The following set of policy propositions derived from our review of research on child development is most directly linked to the focus of that review—namely, *the family*. Before going into these propositions, a few words of caution or clarification are necessary. There is a danger that some readers will interpret the propositions as a conservative plea to save the nuclear family at all costs since this is the optimal environment for rearing children. That is *not* the intention of the proposition. In fact, we have not examined literature that could lead to that inference. The research that was reviewed merely identified some characteristics of the most adequate kinds of environment and care for young children. However, it does seem true that *at present in our society* these conditions are most *likely* to occur within families. The "families" may be biological, adoptive, or self-chosen, but are small groups of people committed to the long-term care of their children. We are not claiming anything magical about "the family," but merely noting that in our society it is the most likely environment in which people will be decent and committed to each other and thus provide adequate child care. Research does suggest, however, that when outside pressures and environmental stresses act on the family this has an effect not only on children directly but also on the quality of child care that is provided. Research also shows that the number of families affected by these stressful circumstances—divorce, illegitimacy, urbanization, isolation, fragmentation, working mothers—is increasing from year to year (cf. Bronfenbrenner, 1975). Consequently, our propositions about the family take as their general theme urging, suggesting, and justifying services to provide supports that will help parents raise their children and give them satisfactory care.

7. *A child should be helped to develop a secure attachment to his or her parents, and then, increasingly, be given opportunities to interact with other adults and children*

During the infant's first year of life forming a *secure* "attachment" relation with another person—usually the mother—is important for development. The child's need for such a relationship has several implications for policy. First, we know that a necessary condition for the development of such an attachment is adequate positive, active interaction with a caregiver. We cannot yet specify precisely the limits of what is "adequate"—this would vary from baby to baby and caregiver to caregiver—but within the limits observed in normal families, the relation seems to be that the *more* interaction engaged in with *more* affection and *more* responsiveness the better. This suggests that the person who has primary responsibility for the infant's care (typically the parent or foster parent) should be encouraged to interact with the infant warmly and frequently, particularly when the baby expresses a social or physical need.

There is also evidence that attachment develops more easily if there are *few* caregivers and if the same ones *continue* for a substantial period of time. This is a situation that in our society is most often provided by parents in a stable family. Children who have been observed by researchers developed attachments in the first year most successfully in the environment provided by a small family which had enough time for frequent, regular, consistent, and positive interaction among family members. If parents behaved negatively and unresponsively to the child or if they were seldom available for interaction, secure attachments did not develop. Under the latter circumstances, when family care in the first year is not adequate or available, other arrangements for child care should be made. When an alternative child-care arrangement is used at this age, however, parents should be especially sensitive to the quality of their—limited—interaction with the child and to the quality of the care provided by the substitute caregiver. Because the quality of interaction more than the quantity affects the attachment relation, it is possible that even brief, regular, interactions with parents, as long as they are positive and responsive, may be sufficient for the development of the infant's attachment to the parents. This issue requires further research.

Although it is true that having too many different caregivers is detrimental to the development of optimal attachment, this does not mean that a child is best raised by one person alone. In fact, after a primary attachment relation has been established, it is necessary for further development that the child separate from that person and form other social relations. This is best achieved when the child interacts often with a variety of people. Therefore, after the child has developed a primary attachment in the first year, parents should be encouraged to share the child's care with other adults, to offer the child opportunities to interact with other adults and, later, with other children. Supportive services for families that are socially isolated might well include supplementary part-time child care—babysitters, parents' helpers, family day care, center day care, nursery school, or play groups.

As we have noted, when a strong relationship with the mother or other caregiver has developed, children often react negatively to separations from that person or to strangers who approach the child intrusively or when alone. Whenever separation from the mother is necessary (for example, if she has to work or be hospitalized, or if the child needs to be hospitalized), measures should be taken to minimize the painful effect on the child. This is especially important from about seven months to three years, when effects of such separation are most pronounced. Such measures to alleviate separation distress might include providing adequate substitute care, preferably in the child's own home so he or she is in least familiar surroundings; introducing separation gradually so the child learns that the mother will return; allowing the child to visit the mother in the hospital or vice versa; and not leaving the child alone with a stranger (i.e., the substitute caregiver or babysitter) but having mother stay with them until the child gets to know the other person.

Although most research on the development of attachment has focused on mothers, there is evidence that children also form attachments to their fathers in the first year. There are clear advantages for a child in having two strong social relationships—particularly when circumstances necessitate the mother's absence, as in the reasons listed above. To foster children's attachment to their fathers, therefore, fathers also should be encouraged to participate actively and frequently in positive interaction with their infants.

8. *Policy should also promote the parents' attachment to the baby from the beginning*

Adults, as well as infants, develop strong emotional attachments—one of particular significance being that of a mother to her baby. It is this attachment that allows mothers to tolerate the burdens of child rearing and to provide the loving care essential to children's development. Research suggests that the development of this attachment is associated with the birth, initial contact, and early care of the infant; the reciprocally interactive mother–child system clearly begins at the moment of birth, if not before. This has implications for at least three areas of policy: hospital maternity procedures, daycare arrangements, and employment practices.

To foster mutual mother-infant interaction and attachment, a "rooming-in" arrangement in the hospital, in which the newborn baby stays with the mother and is cared for by her rather than staying in a nursery, is supported by the data and is recommended as hospital policy unless there are prohibiting factors such as ill health or prematurity. The rooming-in arrangement should begin immediately after the birth. To facilitate a strong father–child relationship—and possibly to strengthen the mother–father tie at the same time—we might also propose that fathers "room-in" too. If rooming-in for fathers is unfeasible, hospital visiting hours could provide the father with free access to mother and infant at any time of day or night (family-centered maternity care), whereas visiting by others than those likely to be significantly involved in the child's life would be strictly limited. Not only should mother and father be given free access to the newborn, however, they should also—at least with their first infant—be given some guidance in infant care by the medical staff. Since having mothers care for their infants would relieve nurses of some of their nursery chores, the nursing staff might have more time in a family-centered ward to counsel parents who wanted it.

An alternative to the rooming-in scheme, and one which might have economic advantages for parents, would be to provide supportive services for having babies delivered at home. These deliveries could be performed by professional midwives associated with hospitals. In that way, emergency medical services would be available if needed. Another supportive service might be the provision of inexpensive but trained "mother's helpers" who would aid (but not supplant) mothers during the first few days or weeks postpartum, thus permitting an earlier return home from the hospital and an easier recovery for the mother.

Research on parental attachment has also clear and important implications for parents' use of nonparental day care for their infants. Although the quality and continuity of caregiving in the first three months is not as critical for the *infant's* psychological development as care from then on (i.e., the effects of early deprivation are often reversible), this period may be more critical for the development of the *parent's* attachment to the infant. Consequently, full-time day care in the first three months would not ordinarily be advisable.

Finally, the research on early parent–child attachment has implications for employment practices. In particular, it suggests the value for family relations of maternity and paternity leaves. Leaves from work for both mothers and fathers would, ideally, occur at the same time, following the infant's birth, and last for at least a month for both parents and for at least three months for the parent who was to be the primary caregiver. By this time, the parent would surely be "hooked," and the development of strong bonds between parents and infant well established.

9. *Services should be provided to help parents plan their families and raise their children*

No one family structure is "ideal" for children's development. But it is possible to discuss the likely pros or cons for children in different family structures. The small, intact nuclear family of two parents and two to four children represents the present modal American family. This structure gives children the opportunity to develop an attachment to one or two adults; it gives parents the opportunity to interact often with each child; it allows each parent some help with child care from another adult; and it provides a buffer for unstable or deviant care from one parent, since there is another parent to take over or to provide a balancing influence. The larger extended family, however, has the advantage of providing parents with additional help and guidance with child care, and of providing children with ready access to a variety of different people. Since most families in the United States today are small and without the support of resident relatives, one policy suggestion is that these nuclear families be provided with the additional services ordinarily offered by larger extended families, for instance, supplementary care and social contacts, and, for poor families, "hand-me-down" toys, books, and clothes.

Another suggestion related to family size and structure is that information about and resources for family planning be made more readily accessible to parents and potential parents. Such information could include not only medical advice about birth control, but also information about the *costs* of having children—monetary, practical, and psychological—as well as about the rewards and joy that children can provide. Guidelines for counseling on family size and composition might be derived from research showing that a small family with spacing of at least 3 or 4 years between children may be most encouraging to children's development, because of possible withdrawal, lack of, or competition for parental attention in a large family of closely spaced siblings; or even from research suggesting the advantages of boy–girl sibling combinations for the development of both children's nonstereotyped sex roles. Such counseling naturally would be done on an individual basis, taking into account the clients' personal and cultural values and goals. It would include examination of the clients' motivation for having children, and provision of information that would let them realistically appraise the costs and benefits of having children, so they could make an intelligent and informed decision about having children, when, and how many. Such a counseling service could be particularly valuable for young adults.

There is also research on the *parental* structure of families, which seems to suggest that for children's development, family functioning and climate are more important than the number of parents *per se*. The *lack* of a father (or mother) is not as bad as *having* a father (or mother) is good. However, in our society, two-parent families generally have advantages over one-parent families in terms of status, monetary resources, and division of labor. Moreover, when a single parent has to be both caretaker and breadwinner, this presents great difficulties that can be alleviated only by services to assist him or her either financially or with child care. In line with the suggestion that we propose multiple solutions to such complex problems, here, we might suggest *both* strategies: income support for single parents in any income redistribution scheme, and "homemaker services" to assist single parents with cleaning, housekeeping, laundry, and cooking, thus relieving the physical burdens of parenting. Many single parents, especially those who are divorced or, until very recently at least, unmarried, also face problems of reduction in social status and activities. They must struggle against resentment of the opposite sex, the ex-spouse, or the child. They must overcome isolation, self-doubt, and overprotection or overpermissiveness toward the child. Supportive services for "parents without partners," therefore, might include: psychological or psychiatric counseling to counteract hurt or rejection, social activities (parties, discussions, group activities, etc.) to alleviate loneliness, consciousness-raising activities with other parents without partners, and counseling or help (parent aides) directly oriented toward child care. If the single parent can share the burden of child care with another adult—who is not necessarily a spouse or even of the opposite sex—it will benefit both parent and child. For the parent, it provides relief from the tedium of child care and consultation about child-related problems; for the child, it may break a too-intense bond with the parent, and it provides another role model—another adult to interact with.

As we have just suggested, there are difficulties for parents and children associated with the single parent family. Raising children is a difficult and consuming task—and more so for one person than for two. Problems are more common in one-parent families and more difficult to overcome; such families need extra support. As well as proposing services to assist single parents, therefore, we should also think of ways of preventing families from breaking up unnecessarily, of supporting families in crisis. More ready access for parents to marital counseling services may be one way. This could be accomplished by making marital counseling a tax-deductible expense, by including it in the coverage of insurance or health plans, or by giving or increasing government subsidies to marital therapy clinics (for example, in Community Mental Health Centers). Another preventive measure would be to revise or avoid welfare regulations that make it more profitable for a family to live apart—or to fake living apart. A third strategy would be to give priority to parents with young children or parents in conflict when measures to relieve environmental stresses are recommended or enacted. These measures might include job training and job satisfaction programs, guaranteed income programs, promotion systems, and housing programs. Finally, we might increase public awareness about birth control, abortion, and adoption options for married as well as unmarried parents.

The intention of the proposition and these suggestions about family counseling and family support, it must be stressed once more, is not to "preserve the institution of marriage" and "save the nuclear family," but rather to provide a variety of services to ease the stresses of parenting, prevent unnecessary family breakups, and allow parents of young children to *choose* whether to rear their children together or apart. Our primary goal, here, and elsewhere, is the provision of the best environments for the care of young children.

In the interests of that goal, other strategies for supporting families so they can better care for children can also be envisioned or devised. These, even more clearly than those already suggested, are beyond the domain of the research on child care that was reviewed. They are offered merely as some tentative suggestions of possible strategies for family support. We have no evidence for their relative effectiveness or feasibility—but would propose that all such possibilities be investigated, and then that those which are successful ultimately be made available to all parents who wish or need them.

DAY CARE.   Although it is often viewed as a threat to family integrity, day care can also be seen as a support service for families. Specific suggestions for day-care policy and practice are discussed in a later section. Here, we would just point out that day care—of a variety of forms—can provide a valuable, indeed, often necessary, resource for families in which parents cannot or will not provide adequate and continuous child care.

TEMPORARY (CRISIS) CHILD CARE.   Such care often could be used even by normally well-functioning families; for example, when the mother is hospitalized. If adequate substitute care during this period is not available, children may suffer. Agencies might be established to provide trained substitute caregivers (like substitute school teachers) who would go into the child's home or, if necessary, take the child into their own home, on a temporary basis.

CHILD–FAMILY SCREENING.   Especially for parents who are worried about the progress of their child or the adequacy of their child care, a diagnostic screening service could provide support as well as evaluation. In addition to assessing children's development, and pointing out any problems in their intellectual, physical, or psychological development, the screening could include assessment of the child's social and material environment and identification of any major deficiencies there. Such a service could be made available and encouraged on a regular basis from the time a woman became pregnant until the children were grown.

CHILD-DEVELOPMENT SPECIALISTS OR CHILD-CARE COUNSELORS. These would be concerned and qualified adults who, at the request of the family or some other agency such as the school or a pediatrician, could observe· family dynamics, provide a neutral setting for discussion of child-rearing problems among family members, and offer advice about solutions when asked. They would be neither social workers nor family therapists (although their training might be similar to those professionals), but a resource for normal families with difficulties or problems. Such problems might arise with the birth of a new baby, for example. A good way to introduce the service, therefore, would be in the hospital at the time of birth (or adoption) of the baby. Women suffering a depressive postpartum reaction might very well find the child-care counselor a valuable resource. Such counselors would not regard the family as "ill," would not be evaluating the family or controlling the welfare check; they would attempt to increase rather than undermine parents' confidence and competence.

HOMEMAKER SERVICES. These services would include cleaning, cooking (e.g., "meals on wheels"), laundering, child care, and occasional babysitting to relieve parents of some of the *physical* burdens of parenting. Services now available only for the affluent could be subsidized for middle- and low-income families by providing inexpensive help with such activities. Teenagers and senior citizens might be available to work as such "house-helpers" or "family aides."

FAMILY RESOURCE CENTER. A particularly interesting, but untested proposal—the family resource center—could be a place in the neighborhood, a telephone "hotline," a series of special public programs, or all of these. Its aim would be to offer a centralized service for all families, not just poor ones. Such a resource center might provide:

—information about local schools and day-care facilities (costs, admission criteria, evaluative descriptions, locations)
—diagnostic screening and testing of children
—access to other community social services, including referrals for therapy or health care, counseling for divorce, marital conflict, child custody, or family-planning
—educational programs for parents or expectant parents in

child-care skills, nutrition, homemaking, consumerism, home repairs, etc.

—help in organizing parent groups or cooperative child-care facilities (day care, playgroups, babysitting cooperatives, etc.)

—advice concerning legal rights of parents, children, and families

—adoption and foster care referrals

—information about income supplements, food stamps, housing, etc.

—a welcome service for new neighbors

—organization or provision of temporary crisis care or occasional day care for children

—toy/book/film/curriculum library, particularly for materials for and about children and child care

—a service for child abuse—reporting, treatment, preventive programs

—training programs for child-care workers (family helpers, parent aides, day-care workers)

—organization or provision of homemaker services (laundry, meals-on-wheels, etc.)

10. *Support services, work practices, and income maintenance should be provided for mothers to choose whether they want to work or to stay home*

Mothers of young children, in larger and larger numbers, are going to work—and will probably continue to do so. One survey shows, however, that even when mothers are working they still spend about the same amount of time on child care as when they are not employed. The outcome of this practice is probably often less adequate care—as mothers are tired from working all day—and less adequate work—since mothers still have to worry about parental and household responsibilities while on the job. It has also been observed that mothers who work are less able than those who do not work to participate in educational programs with their children. Policies to alleviate mothers' double burden would seem to be in order. These might include (a) provision of adequate services for supplementary child care (day care, etc.); (b) shorter work hours for mothers *and* fathers; (c) more opportunities for part-time employment for those who want it; (d) creative work schedules that permit extended periods off for parenting in the first few years of a child's life—"work now, nurture later" or "nurture now, work later" schemes—and reentry and retraining opportunities for parents who take advantage of such schemes; and (e) income support for mothers who wish to stay at home but cannot afford to. Since empirical data suggest that a mother's satisfaction with her role, whether it be at home or in the work force, is related to her behavior toward her children, giving women the option of staying home or working may be one way of increasing the likelihood of positive parenting. It should be noted, however, that the data for this generalization are merely correlational, and therefore, although it makes intuitive sense, the assumption that maternal role satisfaction necessarily leads to more positive child care is not strictly empirically based.

11. *Fathers should be encouraged to spend more time parenting and to adopt a more nurturant role if they choose to*

The literature on families suggests that fathers are an underutilized resource for child care. When given the opportunity, many fathers are willing and able to interact with their infants and young children—but in "real life" apparently they seldom do. As women are entering the work force in greater numbers and, consequently, are less available as full-time caregivers, since children benefit from close relations with fathers who are accepting, nurturant, playful, and stimulating, and because a balance between the roles of mother and father (in which neither parent dominates the affection or discipline of the child) is beneficial for children's development, policies that allow and encourage fathers to take a more active role in caring for their children are indicated. Such policies need to be explored on a number of levels. First, we might explore ways of promoting a change in the attitude and values of American society so that such nurturing care would be perceived as appropriate for men to give as well as women. A public campaign might show how skilled men can be at caring for children in day-care centers, as babysitters, as "big brothers," as single parents, and in two-parent families in which the mothers work, for instance. Such a campaign could also stress the subjective experiences—of fun and frustration—for such male caregivers and the benefits of treating child care as a joint, cooperative venture between parents. A number of TV programs on the subject have already been aired, and some magazines now regularly include articles about fathers' experiences. These may reflect a promising trend toward increased participation of men in child care.

On a different level, classes in high school on child development, family life, or preparation for parenthood, should actively recruit and appeal to boys as well as girls. Similarly, prenatal classes for expectant parents, or postnatal programs for first-time parents, could include more information directed specifically to men—supporting, guiding, instructing, and preparing them for fatherhood. Hospital policies that allow the participation of fathers in the birth and early care of the infant could be encouraged more widely. This does seem to be a current trend, but there are still many hospitals that exclude fathers from the delivery room and impose restricted visiting hours. Finally, and perhaps most important, work schedules that allow fathers more time for their families could be explored (paternity leaves, etc.).

As well as generally spending less time with their children, fathers tend to behave differently from mothers when they do interact with their children. With preschool and school-aged children, mothers, traditionally, have been observed to be more expressive, warm, accepting, nurturant, and positive; fathers, more distant and controlling. To the extent that these different patterns of parental behavior are accurate and are the result of parents' behaving in sex-role stereotyped ways—because they think they're *supposed* to—programs or policies which would counteract such stereotypes and demonstrate increased role options would be valuable. Educational programs for parents might well include suggestions for fathers that encourage them to express their affection for their children and participate more in nondisciplinary caregiving. It is not necessary, or even desirable, however, that mothers and fathers behave identically toward their children. Observation of some variety in adult roles and behavior—if not vastly unbalanced or inconsistent in intention—is beneficial for children's development. Moreover, families, like small groups, may be more productive or harmonious when they have a "social leader" and a "task leader." What should perhaps be avoided, however, is the parents' assumption of markedly different responsibilities and rigid roles strictly on the basis of sex identity. It is perfectly reasonable that in some families the father might feel more comfortable with and therefore assume the relatively more nurturant role.

One of the critical ways in which mothers and fathers differ in their treatment of children is in the area of sex-role development. It has been observed that fathers tend to differentiate more sharply than mothers in their behavior toward girls and boys and in what they consider appropriate activities for each. If this means, as it often does, that fathers do not encourage boys to be expressive and nurturant or girls to be thoughtful and achieving, then any programs that promote the "liberation" of fathers' attitudes and behavior should be recommended.

12. *Parent education programs should be improved and made available to all parents and prospective parents who want them*

Even if it were possible to relieve all environmental stresses, redistribute income equitably, and provide adequate wages, housing, health care, day care, legal care, consumer protection, schools or non-schools for all families, there would still be intrafamilial and interpersonal conflicts and inadequacies, and consequently a place for educational or therapeutic programs for parents. Here, we discuss various formats such programs might adopt.

Unfortunately, we do not yet know very effective ways of providing educational experiences to enhance parenting skills; we do know that some strategies are relatively less effective (cf. Bronfenbrenner, 1974; Horowitz & Paden, 1973). Group education programs for parents, such as lecture and group discussions—even if their children are involved, but especially if they are not—do not particularly attract parents, particularly less affluent, single, working parents with large families or personal problems. Nor are programs as likely to be attractive if parents are contacted by the school or agency rather than initiating that contact themselves. Moreover, programs which attempt to change parents' attitudes are typically not effective in producing that change. It is not surprising that any program, especially a discussion or lecture-type program, does not cause a radical shift in parents' feeling or attitude toward their children. Such profound changes are likely to evolve only gradually through experiencing repeated, rewarding interaction with the child. Similarly, simply *telling* a mother to change her attitude, feeling, or behavior does not produce marked change. At the very least, *demonstration* of the desired behavior, particularly of a more complex behavior, in *interaction* with a child is necessary.

The possibilities of preparental education courses in child development and family life as part of the high school curriculum have not been explored in depth. Particularly if accompanied by extensive practical experience with real children and real family problems, this would seem to be a promising way of reaching and educating prospective parents before the real burdens of parenting descend and before firm attitudes toward one's own children are established. Field experience could be gained in day-care or babysitting settings, with pupils' own families, or by simulated incidents in the classroom. Similar experiences could also be offered in adult education courses in child care and development, in prenatal programs for expectant parents, or at the "family resource center" described earlier. Another medium for parent education that deserves further exploration is television; creative programming here could effectively inform and advise parents about child-care skills.

Judging by results of past educational attempts to enhance the quality of parental child care, programs with the greatest probability of success in attracting parents and changing their behavior would likely involve:

—neighborhood or, better, home-based instruction
—parents' active involvement and participation in teaching or interacting with their own children
—specific, focused, interactional educational experiences for each child, presented individually, in a one-to-one situation
—goal-specific curricula (to date, curricula aimed specifically at children's cognitive or language skills have been most effectively communicated to parents. Curricula should be extended to include experiences that demonstrate to parents the need for being responsive to children's behavior as well as stimulating their senses)
—projects determined, planned, and carried out by parents themselves
—relatively long-term programs that continue instruction and maintain support
—small, intensive programs with a research/evaluation component

In general, it also seems likely that the optimal timing for such programs would be from the prenatal period through the first two or three years of the child's life. As well as being an important period in the child's development, this is a critical time for parents, a time in which they develop expectations about infants and parenting and find out if they were realistic, form initial attitudes toward the child, and evolve strategies and patterns of caregiving.

Alternative Child-Care Environments

Although the research reviewed for this report was restricted to investigations of relations between children's development and *family* care, implications of that research can also be drawn for other care institutions or arrangements. Two, in particular, are relevant and discussed in this section: day care (supplementary care) and adoption or foster care (substitute care).

13. *A wide variety of "quality" day-care arrangements should be provided to accommodate the needs of different parents and children*

The decision as to whether or not to put a child in a nonparental day-care arrangement must be based on parents' evaluation of conditions in the family and in available day-care settings. Although some research (on the development of mutual attachments between parents and children) suggests that it may be preferable for children under three years, and especially in the first year, to be cared for at home by a willing and competent parent, some kind of day care is often necessary if such parental care is not available or adequate. If both parents work, if there is only one parent in the household, if the parents are seriously uninterested in child care or are potentially abusive, if the caregiving parent has some mental or physical handicap, if the family is too large for the parents to care for all the children adequately by themselves—for any of these reasons, placement of the child in an alternative or supplementary day-care arrangement seems justified.

The most satisfactory supplementary care arrangement to support the development of children in the first few years would probably be a regular babysitter in the home, since she could most easily provide the continuous, individualized attention needed by the young child. If this arrangement were not available, a family day-care home or a developmental day-care center might also provide care which was supportive of young children's development. In general, unless circumstances dictate otherwise, it seems advisable to delay nonparental day care at least until the parent has formed an attachment to the infant (three months), preferably until the child has formed an attachment to the parent (1 year), and then, if possible, until the "peak" of attachment has passed ($1\frac{1}{2}$ to 2 years). Some evidence also suggests that it may be advisable to delay full-time care in a day-care *center* until the child is three years old and able to cope more easily with the conditions of group care.

When the young child is to be placed in a day-care arrangement, however, there are certain recommendations for maximizing the "quality" of that day care that can be extrapolated from research on the effects of different kinds of child care in families, and which can guide day-care policy and practice and parents' choice of day-care setting. These recommendations follow.

CONSISTENCY OF CARE.   Research on the effects of inconsistency between parents suggests that it would be beneficial if care in the day-care arrangement were internally consistent and consistent with the parents' behavior, values, and desires.

CONTINUITY OF CAREGIVING.   Research on attachment indicates that children at home thrive when there are a few adults who care for them continuously for a substantial period of time. Temporal stability is a criterion that should be satisfied by day care as well as family care. The child should be placed in a single day-care setting for a relatively long time, where staff members are relatively stable, and continuous care by the same caregiver can be provided. Although a change may be "as good as a rest," too many changes definitely are not—especially for young children.

ASSIGNMENT OF CAREGIVERS TO CHILDREN.   The literature on the development of children's attachments to adults suggests the desirability of children's developing close relationships with a few persons during the first year of life, relationships which will continue to be important during the next couple of years. If a child is placed in day care or with a substitute caregiver within the first year of life, such relationships may develop with the adults providing day care. Consequently, to encourage that possibility, it is suggested that a small number of persons be primarily responsible for the care and entertainment of any individual infant in day care. For children under two years it might be a good practice to assign caregivers to individual children rather than by task. This would allow the caregivers to get to know individual children intimately, and thus be able to respond more accurately to their expressions, thereby increasing the chances for development of such close social relationships and of the children's intellectual skills as well.

ADULT–CHILD RATIO. Clearly, a sufficient number of adults in day care, as at home, is a necessary condition for adequate care and attention for individual children. Some minimum adult–child ratio standard for day care should therefore be supported, especially for very young children. Children need ample numbers of qualified adult caregivers. Unfortunately, for those who would legislate "quality" day care by establishing adult-child ratio standards, however, all caregivers, like all parents, do not give equally good care. Adult-child ratios can only define the *lower* limits of adequate care. This is why standards for hiring and training individual caregivers that focus on the caregivers' ability to interact with children are also necessary.

SELECTION OF CAREGIVERS. Selection of persons to work in day-care settings and procedures for training such persons can be guided by good sense and empirical information on adequate child care by parents. Liking for and an interest in children would seem to be primary prerequisites for hiring. Especially for younger children, the affection, nurturance, and sensitivity of the adult caregiver are paramount. An awareness of children's developing skills, and a willingness to listen to the child and to adapt one's expectations and behaviors to the child's level and needs, are also valuable. It seems less likely that these qualities would be displayed in an interview or written examination for screening prospective caregivers, or be indicated by a college degree or other credential, than that they would show up in interaction with children. Observational screening techniques for hiring should, therefore, be explored and refined.

PREPARATION OF CAREGIVERS. Although certain qualities of excellent caregivers are, of course, not trainable, some specific skills and basic knowledge about child development can be imparted in educational programs. It may be inferred from the research on child care in families that actual interaction with children is a more valuable part of such education than "book learning."

APPROPRIATE DISCIPLINE. Research on families clearly demonstrates that harsh, severe, and frequent punishment is detrimental to children's development. Such disciplinary practices must be avoided in day care, as well as at home. The optimal disciplinary strategy seems to be one which sets rational, appropriate, and clearly defined limits, and enforces them reasonably and gently, although firmly. Such a strategy would be well advised in a day-care program—not only as an effective and benign method of discipline from the child's point of view, but because it is the one strategy most likely to be convincing to a *variety* of parents and, to some degree, at least, consistent with their own practices at home.

SAFE, STIMULATING ENVIRONMENT. As well as suggesting criteria for the human environment in day care, the research on children and families supports the notion that children benefit from freedom to move and explore in a safe and stimulating physical environment. This can be interpreted in terms of adequate space and appropriate materials for each child. The finding of a relationship between children's development and the mediation or adaptation of materials by the caregiver may be even more important, however; and further supports the merits of high staff ratios in day care. Because resources for day care are nearly always limited, it is often necessary to assign priorities to expenditures. One implication we would draw from the research on child development is that although space and materials are desirable, the price for safety and an adequate number of adults should be assured first.

SIZE AND COMPOSITION OF GROUPS. Extrapolating from research on family size and spacing, it appears that there may be advantages for younger children in being cared for in relatively small groups (as would occur naturally in a family or day-care home) and/or of having the composition of those groups heterogeneous by age (again, like the situation in a family). Heterogeneous grouping would increase the likelihood that younger children would learn from older ones, while older children would have more responsibility and more opportunity for nurturing. This practice might be particularly valuable when the adult-child ratio is low.

GRADUAL ADMISSION.   In the first two years of life, children raised at home are often anxious or upset when separated for the first few times from their mothers or other principal caregivers, especially in a strange place and when approached by strangers. This generalization has implications for admission procedures in group day care: (1) Separation might be less painful if children were introduced to the day-care setting gradually, not all-at-once-for-the-entire-day. (2) Experience with unfamiliar adults at home prior to admission to day care could dilute the distress of suddenly being cared for by strangers. (3) At first, the unfamiliar persons in the day-care setting might behave receptively but not intrusively or aggressively toward the child and not come between the child and his or her mother. (4) The initial adjustment of the child could be eased by the presence of the mother. When mother is present, the unfamiliar is interesting and explorable; when she is away, it may be frightening. Therefore, mothers might remain with children in day care until they become familiar with the place and with the strange new people. (5) A "readiness" criterion for leaving a child in the day-care center only when he or she is not unconsolably distressed by separation or by the situation might be established. (6) A policy of open admission to day care year-round has the advantage of letting caregivers get to know and understand a few children at a time. It also allows individual mothers to be present in the day-care center during the child's period of adjustment without undue crowding and confusion.

RELATION TO FAMILY.   Day care can offer all parents and, in fact, all adults, valuable avenues of involvement with children—through learning, playing, and working in the center; it should be treated as a route to strengthening not diluting family relations. Particularly for single parents, day care provides an important service. It not only provides essential supplementary or substitute care for the child, but it can increase the parent's competence as a caregiver at home by alleviating the worry, hassle, and fatigue of constant child care, and by supporting positive and educational experience with his or her own child and other children in the day-care program. It can also offer parents an opportunity for meeting and sharing with other parents who have similar experiences and problems. Day-care facilities should welcome parents and encourage them to visit the children and meet with other parents or teachers at all times.

STAFF SATISFACTION.   If the people who work in day care are to feel enthusiasm and satisfaction with their contribution to the growth of children—which is undoubtedly necessary for their long-term commitment to the job and their pleasant behavior to the children— enjoyable working conditions in day care must be promoted. Measures to enhance day-care positions might include better salaries and benefits, regular raises, systematic skill-based promotions, short work hours, schedules that offer relief from the children and frequent interchange with other adults, and in-service educational opportunities to increase competence and confidence.

The foregoing are some of the suggestions for day care that can be derived from research on child care in families. They have concentrated, for the most part, on day care for children in the first three years of life. Once again, in the context of day-care practice and policy, it is crucial to underscore that children at particular ages have different capacities and needs. The salience, continuity, and stability of a few nurturant caregivers is important in the first few years of life, but less so later. A variety of adults in day care can and should be introduced gradually, after the child has established early attachment relations. With older children, the supervised contact with other children and the opportunity for independent experience with stimulating materials that day care can provide take on greater importance, and should, perhaps, be stressed.

14. *Policy should encourage adoption rather than foster care, early rather than late adoption, and adoption by adults who are or can be competent caregivers*

The potential advantages of the biological family as a child-rearing environment—the long-term commitment of its members, the postpartum hormonal factors influencing maternal behavior, the earlier opportunities of natural mothers for extended contact with their newborns, and the more probable temperamental compatibility and intellectual similarity of children with their natural parents—cannot be ignored. Nor can the problems of adoption—the waiting, the difficulty of matching children with parents, the question of what to tell a child about his parentage, and the problematic feelings of the child toward both sets of parents. However, in reality, for a variety of reasons, not all parents are able to fulfil their potential child-rearing role. Therefore, supplementary or substitute care must sometimes be provided on a permanent or short-term basis. The guiding principle should then be to find "good care" for the child. It is clear that such good care is difficult to find in residential institutions. The most popular and successful strategy currently, therefore, is to place children in adoptive (permanent) or foster (short-term) homes.

Children's need for stability and continuity of care, which has been discussed, strongly suggests a system of early adoption rather than series of short-term foster placements. Foster care, on a temporary basis, should be considered only if attempts are being made concurrently to alleviate the conditions in the home or the problems with the child that precipitated the placement. An endless series of foster placements does not provide a satisfactory alternative to adoption.

Research on the development of parental attachment also leads to a proposition about adoption or foster care. To establish a strong parent-child attachment it is probably best that the adoptive or foster parent be given the infant as soon as possible—preferably immediately after birth. This strategy does not seem unreasonable, since there are more would-be adoptive parents than available infants. If adoptive parents were willing to take an infant before it had been thoroughly screened this might have benefits for subsequent attachment and interaction.

Once the decision has been made for a child to be adopted, the research on child care can help again by identifying certain characteristics of adoptive parents that are likely to maximize the chances that the placement will benefit the child. These include the parents' desire for a child, their liking for children, their experiences with children, and their style of interacting with children. Less important criteria would seem to be the parents' age, religion, occupation, education, or fertility. The challenge for the practitioner, of course, is how to reliably detect, measure, or ensure the former kinds of desirable qualities. Efforts to devise assessment techniques, including observational measures to screen potential adoptive parents, and attempts to design parent education programs for these adults that will enhance positive interactive styles and effective caregiving skills, seem worthwhile and should be supported.

The issue of whether to match children and adoptive parents on the dimension of race or ethnicity is a knotty one. Cultural compatibility with the adoptive parents may make it easier for children to develop a strong sense of cultural identity—a goal which is becoming increasingly important and popular in our pluralistic society. But it may not be as critical for development of ethnic identity or for adjustment in general that the adoptive parents be from the same racial or ethnic group as the child, as it is that they *support* the child's ethnic identity—whatever it is. This area needs further investigation via research rather than rhetoric.

Further suggestions for policy that follow from the perceived benefit of adoption over foster or institutional care are (1) to make adoption easier for prospective parents that are now being screened out, if they meet the behavioral and attitudinal criteria suggested above; (2) to offer adoption subsidies to people who would like to adopt children and who would probably make good parents but who cannot afford it, in order to find families for all homeless children; and, perhaps most important; (3) to establish postadoption follow-up procedures which would enhance the caregiving skills of adoptive parents. In particular, one might think of regular visits for observation, consultation, and assistance from a "child-development counselor," whose role would not include the authority to remove the child, but who would be a helpful and instructive resource for the adoptive parent. Of course, all the programs, resources, and facilities discussed previously in relation to "families" apply to, and could support, adoptive families as well.

An alternative to placement of children through adoption or foster care, but one which has not been systematically studied, is the provision of supplementary care by a relatively permanent or a crisis-targeted, live-in or daily "child carer." This alternative is now open only to affluent families (the nanny or housekeeper) or sometimes to extended families (the aunt or grandmother). It is an alternative that deserves further exploration, since it could provide adequate child care, at home, for children who might otherwise be given up for adoption—in families, for instance, in which parents are handicapped or potentially abusive or neglectful of their children.

One final kind of adoption arrangement which could be explored is "adoption" by a family of a "grandparent" or "grandparents." Retired, perhaps lonely, older people, particularly those without grandchildren of their own nearby, would often make ideal "child carers" or "foster grandparents"—at least on a part-time basis. This might be another way of finding services otherwise provided by an extended family network. One can imagine benefits of the arrangement for the children, their parents, and the "grandparents."

Accessibility and Authority

15. *Policy should make services available but not dictate their use. Provision of adequate family "supports" is to be preferred to direct or involuntary intervention*

The issue addressed by the final proposition is the very difficult but critically important one of *who* should make policy decisions on child care. At least at the present state of our knowledge, it seems clear that the resolution of that question must rest on logic, good sense, and ethical values rather than social science data. The one relevant point derived from research on the family and child development is that a person's behavior and development seem to be related to his control or his perception of control over the environment, at least to the extent that he can predict or anticipate consequences of his own behavior. This is true for people of all ages. Three-month old infants, for example, benefit when their behavior reliably elicits a response from the caregiver, and adults give children better care and participate more actively in child-care programs when they feel competent, confident, and in control, not coerced. The implication that seems to follow is that decisions about participation in programs, about the use of services, about selecting arrangements for child care should be left up to individual families. Therefore, although policy should create new and support existing child-care services, disseminate information about child care, and provide educational opportunities for parents—it does not follow that specific practices or programs should be required or enforced. Except in the most extreme circumstances participation should be voluntary.

Models for variations in programs, services, and child-care arrangements should probably most appropriately be explored at the national level, since substantial funding and extensive resources would be necessary for such major programmatic research. Such intensive study of planned variation in program models would be advised before any particular programs were implemented. This kind of investigation might occur under the auspices of a new federal office on "Child and Family Services" or a new National Institute for "Child

Care and Development." To keep the administration of services on a reasonable scale, and to maximize the likelihood of responsiveness to the needs of particular communities, *implementation* of programs derived from the federally examined alternative models would probably best be kept at the local (city via state) level. *Utilization* of programs or resources, however, must ultimately be the decision of individual families or employers. Researchers and policy makers can make proposals and offer services, but neither group has the skill or the right to assign individuals to treatments.

A dilemma arises, however, when a child is being abused or neglected in the child-care arrangement in which he or she is placed (either home or day care). In this case, whose responsibility is the welfare of the child? The abusive parent or caregiver? Or does the State have a right to intervene? What are the rights of children versus parents? What are the responsibilities of parents versus the State? Our greatest challenge may be to increase public responsibility for children without destroying the sanctity and privacy of the family or the decision-making power of parents. If a child is suffering physical or psychological harm or severe cognitive or social impoverishment, or is presenting a serious behavior problem, some form of intervention may then be justified. Children have individual rights apart from their parents'. They, too, are entitled to "life, liberty..." and a benign environment. The most effective and psychologically sensible intervention, however, according to any implications that may be drawn from the previous discussion, would seem to be one that provided the needed supports for the family, the day-care arrangement, or the child, *in situ*—financial, environmental, educational, or therapeutic—rather than *removing* the child from the situation and placing him in another institution.

Such intervention may not be possible on a legislative or legal level. Besides the ethical issue of intervening, there are immense problems involved in establishing criteria and guidelines for intervention and in enforcing them once established. The current situation regarding laws for child abuse and juvenile justice illustrates the difficulty of state intervention. In cases of psychological abuse or intellectual neglect—conditions which are even harder to assess or monitor—the problems of intervention might well be insurmountable. Presumably most parents want what is best for their children, at least as long as it is compatible with what is best for them. Apparently, also, most families are sufficiently robust and resilient that parents could take advantage of genuine opportunities to choose the supports they want or need. Consequently, if economic, social, and educational support services were available and readily accessible to *all* parents, and if parents were made aware of the importance of children's early experience and of what constitutes a "good" environment or "adequate" care, then it would not likely be necessary to *impose* interventions. Parents would avail themselves of the services voluntarily. Public education to raise the consciousness and responsibility of the public, in general, and parents, in particular, about the needs and development of children would thus seem desirable, and a more satisfactory strategy than enforced intervention.

VI

Concluding Comments

The need for reliable information about children's development which can inform public policy is vital. This book has attempted to provide some such information by reviewing research on relations between child development and parental care and deriving from that review a number of propositions for child-care policy. To make the leap from child development to policy propositions, however, it was necessary to make assumptions, inferences, simplifications, and generalizations that went beyond empirical data. This was necessary because psychological research has seldom been designed with policy issues in mind. The questions raised by policy makers are frequently researchable, but researchers have seldom taken seriously their challenge. It is our final contention here that research can shed important light on policy issues and that studies should be designed to do so more directly and more often. At the present time we know far less than we need to know in order to derive policies from research on child development. This became very clear as such a task was attempted in this book. The following comments, therefore—directed to my colleagues in research—give some suggestions about topics and strategies for research that could facilitate the planning of child-care policies.

Research data presently available on child development in the family are most helpful for identifying critical components of child care and suggesting how they influence children's development. These data tell us a fair amount about qualities of caregiving; by contrast, they indicate nothing about ways of structuring society so as to permit, support, or enhance such caregiving. Research in this area is needed—research that would examine the relative effects on child care of economic or sociological changes such as income redistribution, job sharing, and parental "sabbaticals," or social services such as family helpers or child-development counselors. The research strategy called for by this kind of investigation would be collaborative between psychologists (for measuring child-care "outcomes") and economists, sociologists, or social workers (for defining structural "inputs").

From the available research on child development in the family we also know something of how early care is related to children's contemporaneous behavior; we know far less about the effects of early experience on later development. More longitudinal research is needed. Of particular interest for policy makers is longitudinal investigation of development when children are placed in dramatically different environments at different ages. Some child development experts claim that it is too late to substantially modify development after children reach two or three years of age. If they have not received adequate care by then, these experts claim, children's future development is hopelessly hindered. These conclusions cannot be inferred from research on children's development in normal families, however—although some of the experts have based their claims on the high predictability of competence from three to six years of age for just such children—since normal family environments are relatively stable and unchanging. Only research that systematically examines every possible means for effecting change at a later age can substantiate such prognostications. Research of this kind, which could provide invaluable information for planners of child-care policies, has not been adequately explored—and should be.

The knowledge about child care which we currently possess is also characterized by a large body of information about one group of caregivers—mothers in small, intact, nuclear, middle-class families, from 1950 to 1970—and little about any other caregivers. These mothers have been by far the most popular subjects of investigation. They represent, however, a limited and increasingly outdated sample of caregivers. Research on child care should obviously be extended to include all kinds of caregivers: other adults (grandparents, fathers, older siblings, babysitters), in other kinds of families (large, extended, single-parent), from other socioeconomic strata, in more recent years.

Fathers are one source of child care increasing in prominence as adult roles and values in our society change, and thus are potential subjects of increasing interest for child-care research. Empirical investigation focusing on the participation of fathers in child care has begun, but generally this research has been limited to viewing fathers in terms of the same categories as have been applied to mothers. Since fathers and mothers undoubtedly have independent roles in children's socialization and perform their caregiving functions differently, we need research that will examine paternal behavior with fresh and original perspectives. From such research we could gain valuable information on the impact of men as primary caregivers (in single-parent or intact families), as supplementary caregivers (for their own or other children), and as links with the "outside" world—information not just on what their effects are on children's development, but on how they produce those effects.

Other forms of child care that are alternatives to maternal care—communal, day care, family day care, babysitting—are also becoming of increasing interest as a result of changing adult roles and family life styles. We need to know not only whether the same generalizations about caregiving apply to nonmaternal care, but also about the effects of children's exposure to two or more concurrent caregiving arrangements (for example, home and center) or to more than one primary caregiver (for example, mother and babysitter). Research on these issues, too, would obviously benefit parents and policy planners.

Another area that needs further research attention before policy implications can be specified is the family as a social network. Within the nuclear family, the relations among parents and siblings, and in extended families, the relations among parents, children, grandparents, aunts,uncles, and cousins, are complicated and need investigation. In the former category we need to know more, particularly about the effects of fathers on mother-child interaction, and the effects of older children acting as supplementary caregivers on their siblings—in order to determine whether it makes sense to involve whole families in child-care programs, rather than just mothers. In the latter category, we need data that go beyond a view of extended families as poor and black and explore this alternative family structure in the relatively affluent. Any research that treats the family network as the unit of investigation would seem likely to provide a more appropriate basis for child- or family-oriented policy than research that focuses exclusively on mother or child.

For wise planning of public policies for child care, we need to look even further than the family unit—to study the impact of characteristics of the society in which the family is embedded. At first, psychologists studying child care investigated correlates of breast versus bottle feeding. After some time and study, they found out that the attitudes and behavior surrounding the specific choice of breast or bottle were more important than the caretaking practice *per se*. Today, they know quite a lot about attitudes and behavior, but perhaps a still broader surround has an as yet unappreciated impact on child development, an impact which may or may not be mediated by parental attitudes and behavior toward the child. We need investigations that will examine variables on all these levels. This brings us to a call, first, for ecological research—research that examines children's total life experiences in natural environments; second, for a broader conceptualization of "environment"—a conceptualization that will include families' history, caste, class, neighborhood, and salient societal institutions or structures; and third, for multivariate procedures—research designs and statistical procedures that can handle such a wealth of complex data.

One of the dimensions of an expanded concept of environment that is becoming increasingly prominent in discussions about child care is culture or ethnicity. Cultural aspects of children's experience clearly need much more empirical exploration; for example, exploration of the variety of child-care environments that can support and maintain children's ethnic identities. We should continue to broaden our research horizons to take into account cultural membership. Social class is another aspect of a broadly defined environment. Studies of this dimension reveal much about the behavioral and psychological correlates, for parents and children, of socioeconomic status. Unfortunately, the policy implications of such research are limited by the fact that SES is a complex measure, combining indicators of income, occupation, and education. Research that separated the contributions of these different components of SES would more directly aid policy planners.

As well as needing research on natural environments, we also need research that assesses the effects of *planned* environments—that is, research that evaluates the effects of specific, implemented child-care policies or programs. The research which has been reviewed here, and which provides the basis for current generalizations on good child care, is of care spontaneously provided by mothers, usually in relatively affluent families. We need to do research to find out if the same generalizations apply when educational programs attempt to modify the behavior of other, perhaps less affluent and educated, parents to more closely approximate this middle-class "ideal." It cannot be assumed without evidence either that it will be possible to profoundly and permanently so modify caregiving behavior through education, or that even if modification is possible, such caregiving will have the desired beneficial effects on children's development. Careful and systematic evaluation should be a part of every new policy or program proposed or implemented. Not only should new policies be evaluated when they are first implemented, but monitoring of policy effects should continue, and, when necessary, such assessments should be used for modifying or reformulating policy.

Particular kinds of child-care policy in need of such empirical assessment, since we know so little about them or their relative effects, are mass parent education programs (via TV, books, articles, etc.), new social services for non-poor families (parent helpers, family aides, child-development counselors), and family-support resource centers. The most satisfactory kind of investigation of these and other policies would involve assessment not only of whether the program "worked" (in this case, for example, changed parents' caregiving behavior), but of by-products or other results in the rest of the family (for example, changes in children's behavior, in communication between parents and other extended family members, in parental work patterns, or in parents' use of other services). Evaluation of the effects of the program on individual children and families as well as on the entire group of participants in the program would also be valuable. Group differences hide individual gains and losses. Since one program is not likely to benefit equally everyone in it, research that examined who benefited, and how, would be helpful to policy developers.

The evaluation of program or policy effects is a particular case of research that "tests" empirical relations observed in correlational studies of natural phenomena. Only such systematic experimental intervention permits unequivocal assignment of causal direction to a relationship. The value of experimental studies, in the laboratory or in field settings, is that they can corroborate relationships observed to occur naturally in real life. The combination of both observation and experimentation is a powerful research method, and an especially important one to be exploited if findings of "basic" child-development research are to be applied to policy.

As well as the extensions and refinements for measuring *caregiving* and its relation to child development that have been suggested, there are also ways that the measurement of *children's* behavior could be augmented to enrich the perspective of policy developers. In the past, the focal outcomes for most studies of the effects of child care have been unfortunately narrow as evaluations of children's competence. Study of the relation of caregiving to strictly intellectual development, particularly as indicated by IQ scores, has been especially common. Another popular approach has been to limit investigation to analyzing parents' influence on children's negative or stereotyped social behavior (especially aggression, dependency, and sex-role typing). Four suggestions for child-development research that could enhance the usefulness of collected data for policy planners are (1) to give more attention to studying behavior that is genuinely important and socially desirable, such as prosocial and moral qualities like generosity, helpfulness, cooperation, and altruism; (2) to accept the challenge of investigating the development of significant kinds of behavior that are complex and as yet unquantified (like creativity, curiosity, and coping), rather than just relying on available standardized tests (like IQ and achievement); (3) to develop and refine multivariate measures of children's overall competence, not just assess isolated individual behaviors; and (4) to distinguish between "pacing" variables and "people" variables—that is, between kinds of behavior that are merely accelerated or decelerated in rate of development by different kinds of care, as opposed to those that reflect significant differences in the kind of person that ultimately develops—and to emphasize the latter.

Continuing the topic of assessing children's development, it might also be pointed out that most child development researchers to date have been concerned with establishing chronological norms for development or with defining "normal" child behavior. Their categories and observations of children, however, have been constrained by their middle-class values, and consequently have led to a limited definition of normalcy. Since we know that many different people emerge from vastly different child-caring environments, all apparently equally prepared for adult life, we suspect there is more than one route to competence, and possibly more than one expression of competence in childhood. Research based on a broader concept of "competence," encompassing unusual children and atypical parents, could also greatly enrich policy planning. Such research beyond statistical norms could explore not only the predictable effects of specific environmental events, but how and why individual "exceptional" children coped with those events. This is a final example of the kind of psychological research that might significantly facilitate the formulation of social policy for child care.

Other examples of research investigations that would be of value in planning child-care policy could, of course, be given; this listing is merely suggestive. It should be sufficient, however, to demonstrate the potential usefulness of psychological research for providing some empirical basis for social policy—a theme which has been followed throughout this book. But the relation between research and policy cuts both ways, and it is this thought which concludes the book. Not only can research influence and contribute to policy, but policy can also affect research—for only when there are policies supporting research can empirical inquiry flourish. The relation between research and policy—like that between parent and child—is symbiotic. In the future, as societal changes and the quest for increased information continue the need for both research and policy, one can hope that the relationship between them will become more clearly and productively interactive and reciprocal. It will demand effort on both sides, for the problems of putting the two perspectives together, as this book amply illustrates, are substantial. But if the effort is successful, our children will be the beneficiaries.

Bibliography

Adams, R. L., & Phillips, B. N. Motivational and achievement differences among children of various ordinal birth positions. *Child Development,* 1972, **43,** 155–164.

Ainsworth, M. D. The effects of maternal deprivation: A review of findings and controversy in the context of research strategy. *Public Health Papers,* 1962, **14,** 97–165.

Ainsworth, M. D. The development of infant-mother interaction among the Ganda. In B. M. Foss (Ed.), *Determinants of infant behavior,* Vol. 2. London: Methuen, 1963. Pp. 67–104.

Ainsworth, M. D. Patterns of attachment behavior shown by the infant in interaction with his mother. *Merrill-Palmer Quarterly,* 1964, **10,** 51–58.

Ainsworth, M. D. Maternal behavior and infant initiative. Paper presented at symposium "Maternal behavior in mammals" organized by the International Union of Biological Sciences, London, July 26–27, 1969.

Ainsworth, M. D. The development of infant-mother attachment. In B. M. Caldwell & H. N. Ricciuti (Eds.), *Review of child development research,* Volume 3. Chicago: University of Chicago Press, 1973. Pp. 1–94.

Ainsworth, M. D., Bell, S. M., Blehar, M. P., & Main, M. B. Physical contact: A study of infant responsiveness and its relation to maternal handling. Paper presented at the meetings of the Society for Research in Child Development, Minneapolis, March, 1971.

Ainsworth, M. D., Bell, S. M., & Stayton, D. J. Individual differences in the development of some attachment behaviors. *Merrill-Palmer Quarterly,* 1972, **18,** 123–144.

Aldrich, C. A., Sung, C., & Knop, C. The crying of newly born babies. III. The early period at home. *Journal of Pediatrics,* 1945, **27,** 428–435. (a)

Aldrich, C. A., Sung, C., Knop, C., Stevens, G., & Burchell, M. The crying of newly born babies. II. The individual phase. *Journal of Pediatrics,* 1945, **27,** 89–96. (b)

Aldrich, C. A., Norval, M. A., Knop, C., Venegas, F., & Bell, H. E. The crying of newly born babies. IV. A follow-up study after additional nursing care had been provided. *Journal of Pediatrics,* 1946, **28,** 665–675.

Altus, W. D. Birth order and its sequelae. *Science,* 1966, **151,** 44–49.

128

Ambrose, J. A. The development of the smiling response in early infancy. In B. M. Foss (Ed.), *Determinants of infant behavior*. Vol. 1. London: Methuen, 1961. Pp. 179–196.

Antonovsky, H. F. A contribution to research in the area of the mother-child relationship. *Child Development*, 1959, **30**, 37–51.

Appleton, T., Clifton, R., & Goldberg, S. The development of behavioral competence in infancy. In F. D. Horowitz (Ed.), *Review of child development research*. Volume 4. Chicago: University of Chicago Press, 1975. Pp. 101–186.

Bakwin, H. Loneliness in infants. *American Journal of Diseases in Children*, 1942, **63**, 30–40.

Bakwin, H. Emotional deprivation in infants. *Journal of Pediatrics*, 1949, **35**, 512–521.

Bakwin, H., & Bakwin, R. M. *Clinical management of behavior disorders in children*. Philadelphia: Saunders, 1960.

Baldwin, A. L. The effect of home environment on nursery school behavior. *Child Development*, 1949, **20**, 49–61.

Baldwin, A. L., Kalhorn, J., & Breese, F. H. Patterns of parent behavior. *Psychology Monograph*, 1945, **58** (3, Serial No. 268).

Banducci, R. The effect of mother's employment on the achievement, aspirations, and expectations of the child. *The Personnel & Guidance Journal*, 1967, **46**, 263–267.

Bandura, A., Ross, D., & Ross, S. A. A comparative test of the status envy, social power, and secondary reinforcement theories of identificatory learning. *Journal of Abnormal Social Psychology*, 1963, **67**, 527–534.

Banikiotes, F. G., Montgomery, A. A., & Banikiotes, P. G. Male and female auditory reinforcement of infant vocalizations. *Developmental Psychology*, 1972, **6**, 476–481.

Bartlett, E. W., & Smith, C. P. Child rearing practices, birth order, and the development of achievement-related motives. *Psychological Reports*, 1966, **19**, 1207–1216.

Baumrind, D. Parental control and parental love. *Children*, 1965, **12**, 230–234.

Baumrind, D. Effects of authoritative parental control on child behavior. *Child Development*, 1966, **37**, 887–907.

Baumrind, D. Child care practices anteceding three patterns of preschool behavior. *Genetic Psychology Monographs*, 1967, **75**, 43–88.

Baumrind, D. Current patterns of parental authority. *Developmental Psychology Monographs*, 1971, **4**, 1–103. (a)

Baumrind, D. Harmonious parents and their preschool children. *Developmental Psychology*, 1971, **4**, 99–102. (b)

Baumrind, D. An exploratory study of socialization effects on black children: Some black-white comparisons. *Child Development*, 1972, **43**, 261–267.

Baumrind, D., & Black, A. E. Socialization practices associated with dimensions of competence in preschool boys and girls. *Child Development*, 1967, **38**, 291–327.

Bayley, N. Research in child development. A longitudinal perspective. *Merrill-Palmer Quarterly*, 1965, **11**, 183–208.

Bayley, N., & Schaefer, E. S. Maternal behavior and personality development. Data from the Berkeley Growth Study. *Psychiatric Research Reports*, 1960, **13**, 155–173. (a)

Bayley, N., & Schaefer, E. S. Relationships between socioeconomic variables and the behavior of mothers toward young children. *Journal of Genetic Psychology*, 1960, **96**, 61–77. (b)

Bayley, N., & Schaefer, E. S. Correlations of maternal and child behaviors with the development of mental abilities: Data from the Berkeley Growth Study, *Monographs of the Society for Research in Child Development*, 1964, **29** (6, Serial No. 97).

Becker, W. C. Consequences of different kinds of parental discipline. In M. L. Hoffman & L. W. Hoffman (Eds.), *Review of child development research.* Volume 1. New York: Russell Sage, 1964. Pp. 169–208.

Becker, W. C., Peterson, D. R., Hellmer, L. A., Shoemaker, D. J., & Quay, H. C. Factors in parental behavior and personality as related to problem behavior in children. *Journal of Consulting Psychology,* 1959, **23,** 107–118.

Becker, W. C., Peterson, D. R., Luria, Z., Shoemaker, D. J., & Hellmer, L. A. Relations of factors derived from parent-interview ratings to behavior problems of five-year-olds. *Child Development,* 1962, **33,** 509–535.

Beckwith, L. Relationships between attributes of mothers and their infants' IQ scores. *Child Development,* 1971, **42,** 1083–1097. (a)

Beckwith, L. Relationships between infants' vocalization and their mothers' behaviors. *Merrill-Palmer Quarterly,* 1971, **17,** 211–226. (b)

Beckwith, L. Relationships between infants' social behavior and their mothers' behavior. *Child Development,* 1972, **43,** 397–411.

Bee, H. L. Parent-child interaction and distractibility in nine-year-old children. *Merrill-Palmer Quarterly,* 1967, **13,** 175–190.

Bee, H. L., Van Egeren, L. F., Streissguth, A. P., Nyman, B. A., & Leckie, M. S. Social class differences in maternal teaching strategies and speech patterns. *Developmental Psychology,* 1969, **1,** 726–734.

Bell, R. Q. Developmental psychology. *Annual Review of Psychology,* 1965, **16,** 1–38.

Bell, R. Q. Stimulus control of parent or caretaker behavior by offspring. *Developmental Psychology,* 1971, **4,** 63–72.

Bell, S. M. The effectiveness of various maternal responses as terminators of crying: some developmental changes and theoretical implications. Paper presented at the meetings of the Society for Research in Child Development, Minneapolis, March, 1971.

Bell, S. M., & Ainsworth, M. D. Infant crying and maternal responsiveness. *Child Development,* 1972, **43,** 1171–1190.

Benson, L. *Fatherhood: A sociological perspective.* New York: Random House, 1968.

Bernal, J. Crying during the first 10 days of life and maternal responses. *Developmental Medicine & Child Neurology,* 1972, **14,** 302–372.

Biller, H. B. A note on father absence and masculine development in lower-class Negro and white boys. *Child Development,* 1968, **39,** 1003–1006.

Biller, H. B. Father dominance and sex-role development in kindergarten boys. *Developmental Psychology,* 1969, **1,** 87–94.

Biller, H. B. Father absence and the personality development of the male child. *Developmental Psychology,* 1970, **2,** 181–201.

Biller, H. B. The mother-child relationship and the father-absent boy's personality development. *Merrill-Palmer Quarterly,* 1971, **17,** 227–242.

Biller, H. B., & Weiss, S. D. The father-daughter relationship and the personality development of the female. *Journal of Genetic Psychology,* 1970, **116,** 79–93.

Bing, E. Effect of childrearing practices on development of differential cognitive abilities. *Child Development,* 1963, **34,** 631–648.

Bishop, B. M. Mother-child interaction and the social behavior of children. *Psychological Monographs,* 1951, **65** (11, Serial No. 328).

Bishop, D. W., & Chace, C. A. Parental conceptual systems, home play environment, and potential creativity in children. *Journal of Experimental Child Psychology*, 1971, **12**, 318–338.

Blanchard, R. W., & Biller, H. B. Father availability and academic performance among third-grade boys. *Developmental Psychology*, 1971, **4**, 301–305.

Bloom, K., & Erickson, M. T. The role of eye contact in the social reinforcement of infant vocalization. Paper presented at the meetings of the Society for Research in Child Development, Minneapolis, April, 1971.

Bossard, J. H., & Boll, E. S. *The sociology of child development*. New York: Harper & Row, 1966.

Bowlby, J. *Child care and the growth of love*. Baltimore: Penguin Books, 1958.

Brackbill, Y. Extinction of the smiling response in infants as a function of reinforcement schedule. *Child Development*, 1958, **29**, 115–124.

Bradley, R. W., & Sanborn, M. P. Ordinal position of high school students identified by their teachers as superior. *Journal of Educational Psychology*, 1969, **60**, 41–45.

Bradshaw, C. E. Relationship between maternal behavior and infant performance in environmentally disadvantaged homes. Doctoral dissertation, University of Florida, 1968.

Brazelton, T. B., Robey, J. S., & Collier, G. A. Infant development in the Zinacanteco Indians of Southern Mexico. *Pediatrics*, 1969, **44**, 274–290.

Breland, H. M. Birth order, family configuration and verbal achievement. *Research Bulletin*, Educational Testing Service, Princeton, 1972.

Bresnahan, J. L., & Blum, W. L. Chaotic reinforcement: A socioeconomic leveler. *Developmental Psychology*, 1971, **4**, 89–92.

Brim, O. G. Family structure and sex role learning by children: A further analysis of Helen Koch's data. *Sociometry*, 1958, **21**, 1–16.

Brodbeck, A. J., & Irwin, O. C. The speech behavior of infants without families. *Child Development*, 1946, **17**, 145–156.

Brody, G. F. Maternal child rearing attitudes and child behavior. *Developmental Psychology*, 1969, **1**, 66.

Bronfenbrenner, U. Socialization and social class through time and space. In E. E. Maccoby, I. M. Newcomb, & E. L. Hartley (Eds.), *Readings in social psychology*. New York: Holt, Rinehart, & Winston, 1958. Pp. 400–425.

Bronfenbrenner, U. The changing American child—A speculative analysis. *Journal of Social Issues*, 1961, **17**, 6–18.

Bronfenbrenner, U. Early deprivation in mammals: A cross-species analysis. In G. Newton & S. Levine (Eds.), *Early experience and behavior*. Springfield, Illinois: Thomas, 1968. Pp. 627–764.

Bronfenbrenner, U. *Is early intervention effective? A report on longitudinal evaluations of preschool programs*. [DHEW Publication No. (OHD) 74–25]. Washington: Department of Health, Education and Welfare, 1974.

Bronfenbrenner, U. The challenge of social change to public policy and developmental research. Paper presented at biennial meetings of the Society for Research in Child Development, Denver, April, 1975.

Bronson, W. C. Early antecedents of emotional expressiveness and reactivity control. *Child Development*, 1966, **37**, 793–810.

Bryan, J. H. Children's cooperation and helping behaviors. In E. M. Hetherington (Ed.), *Review of child development research*. Volume 5. Chicago: University of Chicago Press, 1975. Pp. 127–182.

Buium, N., Rynders, J., & Turnure, J. The early maternal linguistic environment of normal and non-normal language-learning children. Paper presented at the Convention of the American Psychological Association, Montreal, September, 1973.

Burton, R. V. Cross-sex identity in Barbados. *Developmental Psychology*, 1972, **6**, 365–374.

Busse, T. V. Child-rearing antecedents of flexible thinking. *Developmental Psychology*, 1969, **1**, 585–591.

Caldwell, B. M. The effects of infant care. In M. L. Hoffman & L. W. Hoffman (Eds.), *Review of child development research*. New York: Russell Sage, 1964. Pp. 9–88.

Caldwell, B. M. Social class level and stimulation: Potential of the home. *Exceptional Infant*, 1967, **1**, 455–466.

Caldwell, B. M., & Hersher, L. Mother-infant interaction during the first year of life. *Merrill-Palmer Quarterly*, 1964, **10**, 119–128.

Caldwell, B. M., Hersher, L., Lipton, E. L., Richmond, J. B., Stern, G. A., Eddy, E., Drachman, R., & Rothman, A. Mother-infant interaction in monomatric and polymatric families. *American Journal of Orthopsychiatry*, 1963, **33**, 653–664.

Caldwell, B. M., Wright, C. M., Honig, A. S., & Tannenbaum, J. Infant day care and attachment. Paper presented at the Annual Meeting of the American Orthopsychiatric Association, April, 1969.

Carew, J. V. Observed intellectual competence and tested intelligence: Their roots in the young child's transactions with his environment. Unpublished manuscript, Harvard University, 1975.

Casler, L. Maternal deprivation: A critical review of the literature. *Monographs of the Society for Research in Child Development*, 1961, **26** (2, Serial No. 80).

Casler, L. The effects of extra tactile stimulation on a group of institutionalized infants. *Genetic Psychology Monographs*, 1965, **71**, 137–175.

Casler, L. Perceptual deprivation in institutional settings. In G. Newton & S. Levine (Eds.), *Early experience and behavior*. Springfield, Illinois: Thomas, 1968. Pp. 573–626.

Caudill, W. Tiny dramas: Vocal communication between mother & infant in Japanese-American families. Paper prepared for the Conference on Culture & Mental Health, Honolulu, March, 1969.

Cazden, C. B. Environmental assistance to the child's acquisition of grammar. Doctoral dissertation, Harvard University, 1965.

Cazden, C. B. Subcultural differences in child language: An interdisciplinary review. *Merrill-Palmer Quarterly*, 1966, **12**, 185–219.

Cazden, C. B., Baratz, J. C., Labov, W., & Palmer, F. H. Language development in day-care programs. In J. L. Frost (Ed.), *Revisiting early childhood education*. New York: Holt, Rinehart and Winston, 1973. Pp. 377–397.

Chance, J. E. Independence training and first graders' achievement. *Journal of Consulting Psychology*, 1961, **25**, 149–154.

Chilman, C. S. Poor families and their patterns of child care: Some implications for service programs. In L. L. Dittman (Ed.), *Early child care: The new perspectives*. New York: Atherton, 1968. Pp. 217–236.

Chittenden, E. A., Foan, M. W., & Zweil, D. M. School achievement of first- and second-born siblings. *Child Development*, 1968, **39**, 1223–1228.

Chodorkoff, J. R. Infant development as a function of mother-child interaction. Doctoral dissertation, Wayne State University, Detroit, 1960.

Cicirelli, V. G. Sibling constellation, creativity, IQ, and academic achievement. *Child Development*, 1967, **38**, 481–490.

Cicirelli, V. G. The effect of sibling relationship on concept learning of young children taught by child-teachers. *Child Development*, 1972, **43**, 282–287.

Cicirelli, V. G. Effects of sibling structure and interaction on children's categorization style. *Developmental Psychology*, 1973, **9**, 132–139. (a)

Cicirelli, V. G. Sibling interaction and cognitive development. Paper presented at the meetings of the International Society for the Study of Behavioral Development, Ann Arbor, August, 1973. (b)

Clarke, A. D., & Clarke, A. M. Some recent advances in the study of early deprivation. *Journal of Child Psychology & Psychiatry*, 1960, **1**, 26–36.

Clarke-Stewart, K. A. Interactions between mothers and their young children: Characteristics and consequences. *Monographs of the Society for Research in Child Development*, 1973, **38** (6–7, Serial No. 153).

Clarke-Stewart, K. A. Sociability and social sensitivity: Characteristics of the stranger. Paper presented at the biennial meetings of the Society for Research in Child Development, Denver, April, 1975.

Clausen, J. A. Family structure, socialization, and personality. In L. W. Hoffman, & M. L. Hoffman (Eds.), *Review of child development research*. Volume 2. New York: Russell-Sage, 1966. Pp. 1–54.

Collard, R. R. Social and play responses of first-born and later-born infants in an unfamiliar situation. *Child Development*, 1968, **39**, 325–334.

Coopersmith, S. *The antecedents of self-esteem*. San Francisco: Freeman, 1967.

Corah, N. L. Differentiation in children and their parents. *Journal of Personality*, 1965, **33**, 300–308.

Cortes, C. F. & Fleming, E. S. The effects of father absence on the adjustment of culturally disadvantaged boys. *Journal of Special Education*, 1968, **2**, 413–420.

Costello, J., & Martin, J. Studies of parents. Preschool project, Evaluation Report No. 1, Institute for Juvenile Research, Chicago, November, 1971.

Costello, J., & Peyton, E. The socialization of young children's learning styles. Unpublished manuscript, Yale University, 1973.

Cox, F. N., & Campbell, D. Young children in a new situation with and without their mothers. *Child Development*, 1968, **39**, 123–132.

Crandall, V. J., Orleans, S., Preston, A., & Rabson, A. The development of social compliance in young children. *Child Development*, 1958, **29**, 429–443.

Crandall, V. J., Preston, A., & Rabson, A. Maternal reactions and the development of independence and achievement behavior in young children. *Child Development*, 1960, **31**, 243–251.

Crandall, V. J., Dewey, R., Katovsky, W., & Preston, A. Parents' attitudes and behaviors and grade-school children's academic achievements. *Journal of Genetic Psychology*, 1964, **104**, 53–66.

Dameron, L. E. Mother-child interaction in the development of self-restraint. *Journal of Genetic Psychology*, 1955, **86**, 289–308.

Dandes, H. M., & Dow, D. Relation of intelligence to family size and density. *Child Development*, 1969, **40**, 641–645.

Dave, R. H. The identification and measurement of environmental process variables that are related to educational achievement. Doctoral dissertation, University of Chicago, 1963.

Dennis, W. Infant development under conditions of restricted practice and of minimum social stimulation: A preliminary report. *Pedagogical Seminary*, 1938, **53**, 149–158.

Dennis, W. Infant development under conditions of restricted practice and of minimum social stimulation. *Genetic Psychology Monographs*, 1941, **23**, 143–184.

Dennis, W. Causes of retardation among institutional children: Iran. *Journal of Genetic Psychology*, 1960, **96**, 47–59.

Dennis, W. & Najarian, P. Infant development under environmental handicap. *Psychological Monographs*, 1957, **71** (Serial No. 436).

Dennis, W., & Sayegh, Y. The effect of supplementary experiences upon the behavioral development of infants in institutions. *Child Development*, 1965, **36**, 81–90.

Deutsch, C. P. Social class and child development. In B. M. Caldwell & H. N. Ricciuti (Eds.), *Review of child development research*. Volume 3. Chicago: University of Chicago Press, 1973. Pp. 233–282.

Dodd, B. J. Effects of social and vocal stimulation on infant babbling. *Developmental Psychology*, 1972, **7**, 80–83.

Drews, E. M., & Teahan, J. E. Parental attitudes and academic achievement. *Journal of Clinical Psychology*, 1957, **13**, 328–332.

DuPan, R. M., & Roth, S. The psychological development of a group of children brought up in a hospital-type residential nursery. *Journal of Pediatrics*, 1955, **47**, 124–129.

Engel, M., & Wieder, S. Psychological mindedness of 14-month-old boys. Paper presented at the meetings of the Society for Research in Child Development, Minneapolis, March, 1971.

Erlanger, H. S. Social class and corporal punishment in child rearing: A reassessment. *The American Sociological Review*, 1974, **39**, 68–85.

Eron, L. D., Banta, J. J., Walder, L. O., & Laulicht, J. H. Comparison of data obtained from mothers and fathers on childrearing practices and their relation to child aggression. *Child Development*, 1961, **32**, 457–472.

Escalona, S. K. Emotional development in the first year of life. In M. J. Senn (Ed.), *Problems of infancy and childhood*. New York: Josiah Macy Foundation, 1952. Pp. 11–92.

Escalona, S. K. Some determinants of individual differences. *Transactions of the New York Academy of Sciences*, 1965, **27**, 802–816.

Etaugh, C. Effects of maternal employment on children: A review of recent research. *Merrill-Palmer Quarterly*, 1974, **20**, 71–98.

Fauls, L. B., & Smith, W. D. Sex-role learning of five-year-olds. *Journal of Genetic Psychology*, 1956, **89**, 105–117.

Fein, G. G., & Clarke-Stewart, A. *Day care in context*. New York: Wiley Interscience, 1973.

Ferguson, L. R. Origins of social development in infancy. *Merrill-Palmer Quarterly*, 1971, **17**, 119–138.

Finney, J. C. Some maternal influences on children's personality and character. *Genetic Psychology Monographs*, 1961, **63**, 199–278.

Fleener, D. E. Experimental production of infant-maternal attachment behaviors. Unpublished manuscript, Indiana University, 1973.

Fogel, A., & Kaye, K. The effect of infants' "cuddliness" on maternal teaching strategies. Unpublished manuscript, University of Chicago, 1973.

Fowler, W., & Swenson, A. The influence of early stimulation on language development. Paper presented at the biennial meetings of the Society for Research in Child Development, Denver, April, 1975.

Freeberg, N. E., & Payne, D. T. Dimensions of parental practice concerned with cognitive development in the preschool child. *Journal of Genetic Psychology*, 1967, **111**, 245–261.

Freud, A., & Burlingham, D. *Infants without families.* New York: International Universities Press, 1944.

Garbarino, J. A preliminary study of some ecological correlates of child abuse: The impact of socioeconomic stress on mothers. *Child Development*, 1976, **47**, 178–185.

Gardner, D. B., Hawkes, G. R., & Burchinal, L. G. Noncontinuous mothering in infancy and development in later childhood. *Child Development*, 1961, **32**, 225–234. (a)

Gardner, D. B., Pease, D., & Hawkes, G. R. Responses of two-year-old children to controlled stress situations. *Journal of Genetic Psychology*, 1961, **48**, 29–35. (b)

Geber, M. The psychomotor development of African children in the first year and the influence of maternal behavior. *Journal of Social Psychology*, 1958, **47**, 185–195.

Gewirtz, J. L. The course of infant smiling in four child-rearing environments in Israel. In B. M. Foss (Ed.), *Determinants of infant behavior.* Volume 3. London: Methuen, 1965. Pp. 205–248.

Gewirtz, J. L., & Gewirtz, H. B. Stimulus conditions, infant behavior, and social learning in four Israeli childrearing environments: A preliminary report illustrating differences in environment and behavior between the "only" and the "younger" child. In B. M. Foss (Ed.), *Determinants of infant behavior.* Volume 3. London: Methuen, 1965. Pp. 161–184.

Giovannoni, J. M., & Billingsley, A. Child neglect among the poor: A study of parental adequacy in families of three ethnic groups. In S. Chess & A. Thomas (Eds.), *Annual progress in child psychiatry and child development.* New York: Brunner/Mazel, 1971. Pp. 323–334.

Goldberg, S., & Lewis, M. Play behavior in the year-old infant: Early sex differences. *Child Development*, 1969, **40**, 21–31.

Golden, M., & Birns, B. Social class and cognitive development in infancy. *Merrill-Palmer Quarterly*, 1968, **14**, 139–149.

Goldfarb, W. Effects of psychological deprivation in infancy and subsequent stimulation. *American Journal of Psychiatry*, 1945, **102**, 18–33.

Goodenough, F. L., & Leahy, A. M. The effect of certain family relationships upon the development of personality. *Pedagogical Seminary*, 1927, **34**, 45–71.

Gordon, I. J. *Early child stimulation through parent education: A final report.* Washington, D. C.: Children's Bureau, Department of Health, Education, and Welfare, 1969.

Gordon, I. J., & Associates. Reaching the child through parent education: The Florida approach. Edited papers from two symposia presented at the Convention of the American Educational Research Association, February, 1969.

Handolin, B. J. & Gross, P. The development of sharing behavior. *Journal of Abnormal and Social Psychology*, 1959, **59**, 425–428.

Hardy, R. C. A developmental study of relationships between birth order and leadership for two distinctively different American groups. *Journal of Social Psychology*, 1972, **87**, 147–148.

Harlow, H. F. The nature of love. *American Psychologist,* 1958, **13,** 373–385.

Harlow, H. F., & Harlow, M. K. Effects of various mother-infant relationships on Rhesus monkeys' behavior. In B. M. Foss (Ed.), *Determinants of infant behavior.* Volume 4. London: Methuen, 1969. Pp. 15–36.

Harper, L. V. The young as a source of stimuli controlling caretaker behavior. *Developmental Psychology,* 1971, **4,** 73–88.

Hatfield, J. S., Ferguson, L. R., & Alpert, R. Mother-child interaction and the socialization process. *Child Development,* 1967, **38,** 365–414.

Haugan, G. M., & McIntire, R. W. Comparisons of vocal imitation: Tactile stimulation and food as reinforcers for infant vocalizations. *Developmental Psychology,* 1972, **6,** 201–209.

Havighurst, R. J., & Davis, A. A comparison of the Chicago and Harvard studies of social class differences in child rearing. *American Sociological Review,* 1955, **20,** 438–442.

Heathers, G. Emotional dependence and independence in preschool children. Paper presented at the meetings of the Society for Research in Child Development, Detroit, 1951.

Heilbrun, A. B., Harrell, S. N., & Gillard, B. J. Perceived maternal child-rearing patterns and the effects of social nonreaction upon achievement motivation. *Child Development,* 1967, **38,** 267–281.

Heinstein, M. I. Behavioral correlates of breast-bottle regimes under varying parent-infant relationships. *Monographs of the Society for Research in Child Development,* 1963, **28** (4, Serial No. 88).

Herzog, E., & Lewis, H. Children in poor families: Myths and realities. *American Journal of Orthopsychiatry,* 1970, **40,** 375–387.

Herzog, E., & Sudia, C. E. Children in fatherless families. In B. M. Caldwell & H. N. Ricciuti (Eds.), *Review of child development research.* Volume 3. Chicago: University of Chicago Press, 1973. Pp. 141–232.

Hess, R. D. Maternal behavior and the development of reading readiness in urban Negro children. Unpublished manuscript, Stanford University, undated.

Hess, R. D. Parental behavior and children's school achievement. In E. Grotberg (Ed.), *Critical issues in research related to disadvantaged children.* Princeton, New Jersey: Educational Testing Service, 1969.

Hess, R. D., & Handel, G. Patterns of aggression in parents and their children. *Journal of Genetic Psychology,* 1956, **89,** 199–212.

Hess, R. D., & Shipman, V. C. Cognitive elements in maternal behavior. In J. P. Hill (Ed.), *Minnesota Symposia on Child Psychology.* Volume I. Minneapolis: University of Minnesota Press, 1967. Pp. 57–81.

Hetherington, E. M. A developmental study of the effects of sex of the dominant parent on sex-role preference, identification, and imitation in children. *Journal of Personality and Social Psychology,* 1965, **2,** 188–194.

Hetherington, E. M. Effects of paternal absence on sex-typed behaviors in Negro and white preadolescent males. *Journal of Personality and Social Psychology,* 1966, **4,** 87–91.

Hetherington, E. M., & Frankie, G. Effects of parental dominance, warmth, and conflict on imitation in children. *Journal of Personality and Social Psychology,* 1967, **6,** 118–125.

Hieronymus, A. N. A study of social class motivation: Relationship between anxiety for education and certain socio-economic and intellectual variables. *Journal of Educational Psychology,* 1951, **42**, 193–205.

Highberger, R. The relationship between maternal behavior and the child's early adjustment to nursery school. *Child Development,* 1955, **26**, 49–61.

Highberger, R. Maternal behavior and attitudes related to behavior of the pre-school child. *Journal of Home Economics,* 1956, **48**, 260–264.

Hindley, C. Ability and social class. In D. Edge (Ed.), *The formative years: How children become members of their society.* New York: Schocken Books, 1970.

Hoffman, L. W., Rosen, S., & Lippitt, R. Parental coerciveness, child autonomy, and child's role at school. *Sociometry,* 1960, **23**, 15–22.

Hoffman, L. W. Effect of maternal employment on the child. *Child Development,* 1961, **32**, 187–197.

Hoffman, M. L. Power assertion by the parent and its impact on the child. *Child Development,* 1960, **31**, 129–143.

Hoffman, M. L. Parent discipline and the child's consideration for others. *Child Development,* 1963, **34**, 573–588.

Hoffman, M. L. Father absence and conscience development. *Developmental Psychology,* 1971, **4**, 400–406.

Holzman, M. Characterization of the verbal environment provided by mothers for their young children. Paper presented at the meetings of the Society for Research in Child Development, Santa Monica, March, 1969.

Honzik, M. P. Developmental studies of parent-child resemblance in intelligence. *Child Development,* 1957, **28**, 215–228.

Honzik, M. P. Environmental correlates of mental growth: Prediction from the family setting at 21 months. *Child Development,* 1967, **38**, 337–364.

Horowitz, F. D., & Paden, L. Y. The effectiveness of environmental intervention programs. In B. M. Caldwell & H. N. Ricciuti (Eds.), *Review of child development research.* Volume 3. Chicago: University of Chicago Press, 1973. Pp. 331–402.

Hunt, J. McV. Toward the prevention of incompetence. Paper presented at the Convention of the American Psychological Association, Washington, D.C., September, 1967.

Hurley, J. R. Maternal attitudes and children's intelligence. *Journal of Clinical Psychology,* 1959, **15**, 291–292.

Hurley, J. R., & Hohn, R. L. Shifts in child-rearing attitudes linked with parenthood and occupation. *Developmental Psychology,* 1971, **4**, 324–328.

Johnson, M. M. Sex role learning in the nuclear family. *Child Development,* 1963, **34**, 319–333.

Jones, S. J., & Moss, H. A. Age, state, and maternal behavior associated with infant vocalizations. *Child Development,* 1971, **42**, 1039–1051.

Kagan, J. On cultural deprivation. In D. C. Glass (Ed.), *Environmental influences.* New York: Rockefeller University Press, 1968. Pp. 211–250.

Kagan, J., & Moss, H. A. *Birth to maturity.* New York: Wiley, 1962.

Kamii, C. K., & Radin, N. L. Class differences in the socialization practices of Negro mothers. *Journal of Marriage and the Family,* 1967, **29**, 302–310.

Karnes, M. B. *Research and development program on preschool disadvantaged children: Final report.* Washington, D.C.: U.S. Office of Education, 1969.

Katkovsky, W., Crandall, V., & Good, S. Parental antecedents of children's beliefs in internal-external control of reinforcements in intellectual achievement situations. *Child Development*, 1967, **38**, 765–776.

Kennell, J. H., Trause, M. A., & Klaus, M. H. Evidence for a sensitive period in the human mother. In M. H. Hoffer (Ed.), *Parent-infant interaction*. The Hague: Mouton, 1975. Pp. 87–95.

Kessen, W., Fein, G., Clarke-Stewart, A., & Starr, S. Variations in home-based infant education: Language, play, and social development. Final report, OCD Grant No. CB-98. August, 1975. Unpublished.

King, D. L. A review and interpretation of some aspects of the infant-mother relationship in mammals and birds. *Psychological Bulletin*, 1966, **65**, 143–155.

Koch, H. L. The relation of certain family constellation characteristics and the attitudes of children toward adults. *Child Development*, 1955, **26**, 13–40. (a)

Koch, H. L. Some personality correlates of sex, sibling position, and spacing among five- and six-year-old children. *Genetic Psychology Monographs*, 1955, **52**, 3–50. (b)

Koch, H. L. Children's work attitudes and sibling characteristics. *Child Development*, 1956, **27**, 289–310. (a)

Koch, H. L. Sibling influence on children's speech. *Journal of Speech and Hearing Disorders*, 1956, **21**, 322–328. (b)

Koch, H. L. Some emotional attitudes of the young child in relation to characteristics of his sibling. *Child Development*, 1956, **27**, 393–426. (c)

Kohn, M. L. Social class and parental values. *American Journal of Sociology*, 1959, **64**, 337–351.

Korner, A. F. *Some aspects of hostility in young children*. New York: Grune & Stratton, 1949.

Kotelchuck, M. The nature of the infant's tie to his father. Paper presented at the meetings of the Society for Research in Child Development, Philadelphia, April, 1973.

LaFore, G. G. Practice of parents in dealing with preschool children. *Child Development Monographs*, 1945, No. 31.

Lakin, M. Personality factors in mothers of excessively crying (colicky) infants. *Monographs of the Society for Research in Child Development*, 1957, **22** (1, Serial No. 64).

Lamb, M. E. Fathers: Forgotten contributors to child development. *Human Development*, 1975, 245–266.

Landy, F., Rosenberg, B. G., & Sutton-Smith, B. The effect of limited father absence on cognitive development. *Child Development*, 1969, **40**, 941–944.

Laosa, L. M., & Brophy, J. E. Effects of sex and birth order on sex-role development and intelligence among kindergarten children. *Developmental Psychology*, 1972, **6**, 409–415.

Lasko, J. K. Parent behavior toward first and second children. *Genetic Psychology Monographs*, 1954, **49**, 97–137.

Lefkowitz, M. M., Walder, L. O., & Eron, L. D. Punishment, identification, and aggression. *Merrill-Palmer Quarterly*, 1963, **9**, 159–174.

Leifer, A. D., Leiderman, P. H., Barnett, C. R., & Williams, J. A. Effects of mother-infant separation on maternal attachment behavior. *Child Development*, 1972, **43**, 1203–1218.

Lenneberg, E., Rebelsky, F. G., & Nichols, I. A. The vocalizations of infants born to deaf and to hearing parents. *Human Development*, 1965, **8**, 23–37.

Levenstein, P. Cognitive growth in preschoolers through verbal interaction with mothers. *American Journal of Orthopsychiatry*, 1970, **40**, 426–432.

Levin, H., & Sears, R. R. Identification with parents as a determinant of doll play. *Child Development*, 1956, **27**, 135–153.

Levine, J., Fishman, C., & Kagan, J. Social class and sex as determinants of maternal behavior. *American Journal of Orthopsychiatry*, 1967, **37**, 397.

Levy, D. M. *Behavioral analysis*. Springfield, Illinois: Thomas, 1958.

Lewis, H. *Deprived children*. London: Oxford University Press, 1954.

Lewis, M. State as an infant-environment interaction: An analysis of mother–infant behavior as a function of sex. *Merrill-Palmer Quarterly*, 1972, **18**, 95–122.

Lewis, M., & Freedle, R. Mother-infant dyad: The cradle of meaning. Paper presented at a symposium on "Language and Thought," University of Toronto, March, 1972.

Lewis, M., & Goldberg, S. Perceptual-cognitive development in infancy: A generalized expectancy model as a function of the mother-infant interaction. *Merrill-Palmer Quarterly*, 1969, **15**, 81–100.

Lewis, M., & Wilson, C. D. Infant development in lower-class American families. Paper presented at the meetings of the Society for Research in Child Development, Minneapolis, March, 1971.

Lewis, M., Weintraub, M., & Ban, P. Mothers and fathers, boys and girls: Attachment behavior in the first two years of life. Unpublished manuscript, Educational Testing Service, 1972.

Lynn, D. B., & Sawrey, W. L. The effects of father-absence on Norwegian boys and girls. *Journal of Abnormal Social Psychology*, 1959, **59**, 258–262.

Maccoby, E. E., & Gibbs, P. Social class differences in child rearing. *American Psychologist*, 1953, **8**, 395.

McCord, W., McCord, J., & Verden, P. Familial and behavioral correlates of dependency in male children. *Child Development*, 1962, **33**, 313–326.

McGraw, M. B. *Growth: A study of Johnny and Jimmy*. New York: Appleton-Century-Crofts, 1935.

Marshall, H. R. Relations between home experiences and children's use of language in play interactions with peers. *Psychological Monographs*, 1961, **75**, No. 509.

Martin, B. Parent-child relations. In R. D. Horowitz (Ed.), *Review of child development research*. Volume 4. Chicago: University of Chicago Press, 1975. Pp. 463–540.

Messer, S. B., & Lewis, M. Social class and sex differences in the attachment and play of the year-old infant. *Merrill-Palmer Quarterly*, 1972, **18**, 295–306.

Milner, E. A study of the relationship between reading readiness in grade one school children and patterns of parent-child interaction. *Child Development*, 1951, **22**, 95–112.

Minton, C., Kagan, J., & Levine, J. A. Maternal control and obedience in the two-year-old. *Child Development*, 1971, **42**, 1873–1894.

Minturn, L., & Lambert, W. *Mothers of six cultures: Antecedents of child rearing*. New York: Wiley, 1964.

Mitchell, D., & Wilson, W. Relationship of father absence to masculinity and popularity of delinquent boys. *Psychological Reports*, 1967, **20**, 1173–1174.

Moss, H. A. Sex, age, and state as determinants of mother-infant interaction. *Merrill-Palmer Quarterly*, 1967, **13**, 19–36.

Moss, H. A., & Kagan, J. Maternal influences on early IQ scores. *Psychological Reports*, 1958, **4**, 655–661.

Moss, H. A., & Robson, K. S. Maternal influences in early social visual behavior. *Child Development*, 1968, **39,** 401–408.

Moss, H. A., Robson, K. S., & Pedersen, F. Determinants of maternal stimulation of infants and consequences of treatment for later reactions to strangers. *Developmental Psychology*, 1969, **1,** 239–246.

Mummery, D. V. Family backgrounds of assertive and nonassertive children. *Child Development*, 1954, **25,** 63–80.

Mussen, P. H., & Distler, L. Child-rearing antecedents of masculine identification in kindergarten boys. *Child Development*, 1960, **31,** 89–100.

Mussen, P. H., & Parker, A. L. Mother nurturance and girls' incidental imitative learning. *Journal of Personality and Social Psychology*, 1965, **2,** 94–97.

Mussen, P., & Rutherford, E. Parent-child relations and parental personality in relation to young children's sex-role preferences. *Child Development*, 1963, **34,** 589–607.

Mutimer, D., Loughlin, L., & Powell, M. Some differences in the family relationships of achieving and under-achieving readers. *Journal of Genetic Psychology*, 1966, **109,** 67–74.

Nash, J. The father in contemporary culture and current psychological literature. *Child Development*, 1965, **36,** 261–297.

Nelson, K. Structure and strategy in learning to talk. *Monographs of the Society for Research in Child Development*, 1973, **38** (1–2, Serial No. 149).

Nichols, R. C. Parental attitudes of mothers of intelligent students and creativity of their children. *Child Development*, 1964, **35,** 1041–1049.

Nisbet, J. D. *Family environment: A direct effect of family size on intelligence.* London: Cassel, 1953. (a)

Nisbet, J. D. Family environment and intelligence. *Eugenics Review*, 1953, **45,** 31–40. (b)

Nye, F. I., & Hoffman, L. W. *The employed mother in America.* Chicago: Rand McNally, 1963.

Olejnik, A. B., & McKinney, J. P. Parental value orientation and generosity in children. *Developmental Psychology*, 1973, **8,** 311.

Olim, E. G. Maternal language styles and children's cognitive behavior. *Journal of Special Education*, 1970, **4,** 53–68.

Osofsky, J. D., & Danzger, B. Relationships between neonatal characteristics and mother-infant interaction. *Developmental Psychology*, 1974, **10,** 124–130.

Osofsky, J., & O'Connell, E. J. Parent-child interaction: Daughter's effects upon mother's and father's behaviors. *Developmental Psychology*, 1972, **7,** 157–168.

Ottinger, D. R., Blatchley, M. E., & Denenberg, V. H. Stimulation of human neonates and visual attentiveness. *Proceedings, 76th Annual Convention of the American Psychological Association*, 1968, 355–356.

Otto, W. Sibling patterns of good and poor readers. *Psychology in the Schools*, 1965, **2,** 53–57.

Ourth, L., & Brown, K. B. Inadequate mothering and disturbance in the neonatal period. *Child Development*, 1961, **32,** 287–295.

Palmer, F. Learning at two. *Children*, 1969, **16,** 55–57.

Parke, R. D. Family interaction in the newborn period: Some findings, some observations, and some unresolved issues. Paper presented at the meetings of the International Society for the Study of Behavioral Development, Ann Arbor, August, 1973.

Parke, R. D., O'Leary, S. W., & West, S. Mother-father-newborn interaction: Effects of maternal medication, labor, and sex of infant. Paper presented at the Convention of the American Psychological Association, Hawaii, September, 1972.

Parsons, T., & Bales, R. F. *Family, socialization and interaction process.* Glencoe, Illinois: Free Press, 1955.

Payne, D. E., & Mussen, P. H. Parent-child relations and father identification among adolescent boys. *Journal of Abnormal and Social Psychology, 1956,* **52,** 358–362.

Phillips, J. R. Syntax and vocabulary of mother's speech to young children: age and sex comparisons. *Child Development,* 1973, **44,** 182–185.

Poznanski, E., Maxey, A., & Marsen, G. Clinical implications of maternal employment: a review of research. *Journal of the American Academy of Child Psychiatry,* 1970, **9,** 741–761.

Pringle, M. L., & Bossio, V. Early, prolonged separation and emotional maladjustment. *Journal of Child Psychology and Psychiatry,* 1960, **1,** 37–48.

Provence, S., & Lipton, R. C. *Infants in institutions.* New York: International Universities Press, 1962.

Rabin, A. I. Infants and children under conditions of "intermittent" mothering in the kibbutz. *American Journal of Orthopsychiatry,* 1958, **28,** 577–584.

Rabin, A. I. The maternal deprivation hypothesis revised. *Israel Annals of Psychiatry and Related Disciplines,* 1964, **1,** 189–200.

Radin, N. Maternal warmth, achievement motivation, and cognitive functioning in lower-class preschool children. *Child Development,* 1971, **42,** 1560–1565.

Radin, N. Father-child interaction and the intellectual functioning of 4-year-old boys. *Developmental Psychology,* 1972, 353–361. (a)

Radin, N. Three degrees of maternal involvement in a preschool program: impact on mothers and children. *Child Development,* 1972, **43,** 1355–1364. (b)

Radin, N. Observed paternal behaviors as antecedents of intellectual functioning in young boys. *Developmental Psychology,* 1973, **8,** 369–376.

Ramey, C. T., Hieger, L., & Klisz, D. K. Maternal deprivation in infancy: The therapeutic role of response-contingent stimulation. Paper presented at the meetings of the Society for Research in Child Development, Minneapolis, March, 1971.

Rebelsky, F., & Hanks, C. Fathers' verbal interaction with infants in the first three months of life. *Child Development,* 1971, **42,** 63–68.

Reppucci, N. D. Parental education, sex differences, and performance on cognitive tasks among 2-year-old children. *Developmental Psychology,* 1971, **4,** 248–253.

Rheingold, H. L. The modification of social responsiveness in institutional babies. *Monographs of the Society for Research in Child Development,* 1956, **21** (2, Ser. No. 63).

Rheingold, H. L. The effect of environmental stimulation upon social and exploratory behavior in the human infant. In B. M. Foss (Ed.), *Determinants of infant behavior.* Volume 1. London: Methuen, 1961.

Rheingold, H. L. Controlling the infant's exploratory behavior. In B. M. Foss (Ed.), *Determinants of infant behavior.* Volume 2. London: Methuen, 1963. Pp. 171–175.

Rheingold, H. L., & Bayley, N. The later effects of an experimental modification of mothering. *Child Development,* 1959, **30,** 363–372.

Rheingold, H. L., Gewirtz, J. L., & Ross, H. W. Social conditioning of vocalizations in the infant. *Journal of Comparative Physiological Psychology,* 1959, **52,** 68–73.

Rheingold, H. L., & Samuels, H. R. Maintaining the positive behavior of infants by increased stimulation. *Developmental Psychology,* 1969, **1,** 520–527.

Rhine, W. R. Birth order differences, conformity, and level of achievement arousal. *Child Development*, 1968, **39**, 987–996.

Ricciuti, H. N., & Poresky, R. Development of attachment to caregivers in an infant nursery during the first year of life. Paper presented at the meetings of the Society for Research in Child Development, Philadelphia, March, 1973.

Robertson, J. Mothering as an influence on early development. *Psychoanalytic Study of the Child*, 1962, **17**, 245–264.

Robson, K. S. The role of eye-to-eye contact in maternal-infant attachment. *Journal of Child Psychology and Psychiatry*, 1967, **8**, 13–25.

Robson, K. S., & Moss, H. A. Patterns and determinants of maternal attachment. *Journal of Pediatrics*, 1970, **77**, 976.

Robson, K. S., Pedersen, F. A., & Moss, H. A. Developmental observations of dyadic gazing in relation to the fear of strangers and social approach behavior. *Child Development*, 1969, **40**, 619–627.

Rosen, B. C., & D'Andrade, R. The psychosocial origins of achievement motivations. *Sociometry*, 1959, **22**, 185–218.

Rosenberg, B. G., & Sutton-Smith, B. Sibling association, family size and cognitive abilities. *Journal of Genetic Psychology*, 1966, **109**, 271–279.

Rosenberg, B. G., & Sutton-Smith, B. Family interaction effects on masculinity-femininity. *Journal of Personality and Social Psychology*, 1968, **8**, 117–120.

Rosenberg, B. G., & Sutton-Smith, B. Sibling age spacing effects upon cognition. *Developmental Psychology*, 1969, **1**, 661–668.

Rosenberg, B. G., & Sutton-Smith, B. Do siblings really count? A longitudinal analysis. Paper presented at the meetings of the Society for Research in Child Development, Minneapolis, April, 1971.

Rosenberg, B. G., & Sutton-Smith, B. *Sex and identity*. New York: Holt, Rinehart & Winston, 1972.

Rosenhan, D. L. Prosocial behavior of children. In W. W. Hartup (Ed.), *The young child*. Volume 2. Washington, D.C.: National Association for the Education of Young Children, 1972. Pp. 340–360.

Rothbart, M. K. Sibling position and maternal involvement. Paper presented at the meetings of the International Society for the Study of Behavioral Development, Ann Arbor, August, 1973.

Roudinesco, J., & Appell, G. Les répercussions de la stabulation hôpitalière sur le développement psycho-moteur des jeunes enfants. *Seminaire Hôpital de Paris*, 1950, **26**, 2271–2273.

Roy, K. Parents' attitudes toward their children. *Journal of Home Economics*, 1950, **42**, 652–653.

Rubenstein, J. Maternal attentiveness and subsequent exploratory behavior in the infant. *Child Development*, 1967, **38**, 1089–1100.

Rutherford, E., & Mussen, P. Generosity in nursery school boys. *Child Development*, 1968, **39**, 755–765.

Saltz, R. Effects of part-time "mothering" on IQ and SQ of young institutionalized children. *Child Development*, 1973, **44**, 166–170.

Sameroff, A. J., & Chandler, M. J. Reproductive risk and the continuum of caretaking casualty. In F. D. Horowitz (Ed.), *Review of child development research*. Volume 4. Chicago: University of Chicago Press, 1975. Pp. 187–244.

Sampson, E. E., & Hancock, F. T. An examination of the relationship between ordinal position, personality, and conformity: an extension, replication, and partial verification. *Journal of Personality & Social Psychology*, 1967, **5**, 398–407.

Santrock, J. W. Paternal absence, sex typing, and identification. *Developmental Psychology*, 1970, **2**, 264–272.

Santrock, J. W. Relation of type and onset of father absence to cognitive development. *Child Development*, 1972, **43**, 455–469.

Saxe, R. M., & Stollak, G. E. Curiosity and the parent-child relationship. *Child Development*, 1971, **42**, 373–384.

Scarr-Salapatek, S. Genetics and the development of intelligence. In F. D. Horowitz (Ed.), *Review of child development and research*. Volume 4. Chicago: University of Chicago Press, 1975. Pp. 1–58.

Schaefer, E. S., & Aaronson, M. Infant education project: Implementation and implications of the home-tutoring program. In R. K. Parker (Ed.), *The preschool in action*. Boston: Allyn & Bacon, 1972. Pp. 410–436.

Schaefer, E. S., & Bayley, N. Maternal behavior, child behavior, and their intercorrelations from infancy through adolescence. *Monographs of the Society for Research in Child Development*, 1963, **28** (3, Serial No. 87).

Schaefer, E. S., Furfey, P. H., & Harte, T. J. Infant Education Research Project, Washington, D.C. *Preschool program in compensatory education, I.* Washington, D.C.: U.S. Government Printing Office, 1968.

Schaffer, H. R. Objective observations of personality development in early infancy. *British Journal of Medical Psychology*, 1958, **31**, 174–183.

Schaffer, H. R. Changes in developmental quotient under two conditions of maternal separation. *British Journal of Social & Clinical Psychology*, 1965, **4**, 39–46.

Schaffer, H. R., & Emerson, P. E. The development of social attachments in infancy. *Monographs of the Society for Research in Child Development*, 1964, **29** (3, Serial No. 94).

Schenk-Danzinger, C. Social difficulties of children who were deprived of maternal care in early childhood. *Vita Humana*, 1961, **4**, 229–241.

Schoggen, M. An ecological study of three-year-olds at home. Nashville, Tennessee: *DARCEE Papers and Reports*, 1969, 3 (7).

Sears, P. S. Doll play aggression in normal young children: influence of sex, age, sibling status, father's absence. *Psychological Monographs*, 1951, **65** (Serial No. 6).

Sears, R. R. Ordinal position in the family as a psychological variable. *American Sociological Review*, 1950, **15**, 397–401.

Sears, R. R. Relation of early socialization experiences to aggression in middle childhood. *Journal of Abnormal and Social Psychology*, 1961, **63**, 466–492.

Sears, R. R. Development of gender role. In F. A. Beach (Ed.), *Sex and behavior*. New York: Wiley, 1966.

Sears, R. R. Relation of early socialization experiences to self-concepts and gender role in middle childhood. *Child Development*, 1970, **41**, 267–269.

Sears, R. R., Whiting, J. W. M., Nowlis, V., & Sears, P. S. Some child-rearing antecedents of aggression and dependency in young children. *Genetic Psychology Monographs*, 1953, **47**, 135–234.

Sears, R. R., Maccoby, E. E., & Levin, H. *Patterns of child rearing*. Evanston, Illinois: Row, Peterson, 1957.

Seder, J. A. The origin of differences in extent of independence in children: developmental factors in perceptive field dependence. Unpublished Bachelor's thesis,

Radcliffe College, 1957. Cited in H. H. Witkin *et al.*, *Psychological differentiation: studies of development*. New York: Wiley, 1962.

Sells, S. B., & Roff, M. Peer acceptance-rejection and birth order. *Psychology in the Schools*, 1964, **1**, 156–162.

Seltzer, R. J. The disadvantaged child and cognitive development in the early years. Paper presented at the meetings of the Society for Research in Child Development, Minneapolis, March, 1971.

Shaw, M. C. Note on parent attitudes toward independence training and the academic achievement of their children. *Journal of Educational Psychology*, 1964, **55**, 371–374.

Siegel, A. E., Stoltz, L. M., Hitchcock, E. A., & Adamson, J. Dependence and independence in the children of working mothers. *Child Development*, 1959, **30**, 533–546.

Siegelman, M. Loving and punishing parental behavior and introversion tendencies in sons. *Child Development*, 1966, **37**, 985–992.

Skeels, H. M., Updegraff, B., Wellman, B., & Williams, H. M. A study of environmental stimulation: an orphanage preschool project. *Iowa State Studies in Child Welfare*, 1938, **15**, No. 4.

Skodak, M., & Skeels, H. M. A follow-up study of children in adoptive homes. *Journal of Generic Psychology*, 1945, **66**, 21–58.

Smart, S. Social class differences in parent behavior in a natural setting. *Journal of Marriage and the Family*, 1964, **26**, 223–224.

Smelser, W. T., & Stewart, L. H. Where are the siblings? Evaluation of the relationship between birth order and college attendance. *Sociometry*, 1968, **31**, 294–303.

Snow, C. E. Mothers' speech to children learning language. *Child Development*, 1972, **43**, 549–565.

Spelke, E., Zelazo, P., Kagan, J., & Kotelchuck, M. Father interaction and separation protest. *Developmental Psychology*, 1973, **9**, 83–90.

Spitz, R. A. Hospitalism. *Psychoanalytic Study of the Child*, 1946, **2**, 113–117.

Spitz, R. A. *The first year of life*. New York: International Universities Press, 1965.

Spitz, R. A., & Wolf, K. M. Anaclitic depression. *Psychoanalytic Study of the Child*, 1946, **2**, 313–342.

Sroufe, L. A., & Waters, E. The ontogenesis of smiling and laughter: a perspective on the organization of development in infancy. Unpublished manuscript. Institute of Child Development, University of Minnesota, 1975.

Starr, S. Vocabulary and syntax: interconnections in early language. Unpublished manuscript, Yale University, 1974.

Stein, A. H., & Friedrich, L. K. Impact of television on children and youth. In E. M. Hetherington (Ed.), *Review of child development research*. Volume 5. Chicago: University of Chicago Press, 1975. Pp. 183–256.

Stendler, C. B. Possible causes of overdependency in young children. *Child Development*, 1954, **25**, 125–146.

Steward, M., & Steward, D. The observation of Anglo-, Mexican-, and Chinese-American mothers teaching their young sons. *Child Development*, 1973, **44**, 329–337.

Stewart, A. H., Weiland, I. H., Leider, A. R., Mangham, C. A., Holmes, T. H., & Ripley, H. S. Excessive infant crying (colic) in relation to parent behavior. *American Journal of Psychiatry*, 1954, **110**, 687–694.

Stewart, R. H. Birth order and dependency. *Journal of Personality and Social Psychology*, 1967, **6**, 192–194.

Stolz, L. M. *Father relations of war-born children*. Stanford: Stanford Univ. Press, 1954.

Stolz, L. M. Effects of maternal employment on children. *Child Development,* 1960, **31,** 749–782.

Sutton-Smith, B., Rosenberg, B. G., & Landy, F. Father-absence effects in families of different sibling compositions. *Child Development,* 1968, **39,** 1213–1221.

Tasch, R. J. The role of the father in the family. *Journal of Experimental Education,* 1952, **20,** 319–361.

Thoman, E. B., Turner, A. M., Leiderman, H., & Barnett, C. R. Neonate-mother interaction: effect of parity on feeding behavior. *Child Development,* 1970, **41,** 1103–1111.

Thoman, E. B., Leiderman, H., & Olson, J. P. Neonate-mother interaction during breast feeding. *Developmental Psychology,* 1972, **6,** 110–118.

Thoman, E. B., Denenberg, V. H., Becker, P. T., Gaulin-Kremer, E., Poindexter, M. M., & Shaw, J. L. Analysis of mother-infant interaction sequences: a model for relating mother-infant interactions to the infant's development of behavioral states. Unpublished manuscript, Stanford University, 1973.

Thomas, A., Chess, S., Birch, H. G., Hertzig, M. E., & Korn, S. *Behavioral individuality in early childhood.* New York: New York University Press, 1963.

Tizard, B., Cooperman, O., Joseph, A., & Tizard, J. Environmental effects on language development: a study of young children in long-stay residential nurseries. *Child Development,* 1972, **43,** 337–358.

Trapp, E. P., & Kausler, D. H. Dominance attitudes in parents and adult avoidance behavior in young children. *Child Development,* 1958, **29,** 507–513.

Tulkin, S. R. Mother-infant interaction in the first year of life: an inquiry into the influences of social class. Doctoral dissertation, Harvard University, 1970.

Tulkin, S. R., & Cohler, B. J. Child-rearing attitudes and mother-child interaction in the first year of life. *Merrill-Palmer Quarterly,* 1973, **19,** 95–106.

Tulkin, S. R., & Kagan, J. Mother-child interaction in the first year of life. *Child Development,* 1972, **43,** 31–41.

Venar, A. M., & Snyder, C. A. The preschool child's awareness and anticipation of adult sex-roles. *Sociometry,* 1966, **29,** 159–168.

Ventis, W. L. A longitudinal comparison of modes of maternal reinforcement for infant vocalization. Unpublished manuscript, University of Tennessee, undated.

Wachs, T. D., Uzgiris, I. C., & Hunt, J. McV. Cognitive development in infants of different age levels and from different environmental backgrounds: an exploratory investigation. *Merrill-Palmer Quarterly,* 1971, **17,** 283–317.

Wahler, R. G. Infant social attachments: a reinforcement theory interpretation and investigation. *Child Development,* 1967, **38,** 1079–1088.

Wahler, R. G. Infant social development: some experimental analyses of an infant-mother interaction during the first year of life. *Journal of Experimental Child Psychology,* 1969, **7,** 101–113.

Waldrop, M. F., & Bell, R. Q. Relation of preschool dependency behavior to family size and density. *Child Development,* 1964, **34,** 1187–1195.

Walker, K. Time use for care of family members. Use-of-Time Research Project, College of Human Ecology, Cornell University, Working Paper No. 1, September, 1972.

Walters, J., Connor, R., & Zunich, M. Interaction of mothers and children from lower-class families. *Child Development,* 1964, **35,** 433–440.

Walters, R. H., & Parke, R. D. The role of the distance receptors in the development of social responsiveness. In L. P. Lippsitt & C. C. Spiker (Eds.), *Advances in child development.* Volume 2. New York: Academic Press, 1965. Pp. 59–96.

Waters, E., & Crandall, V. J. Social class and observed maternal behavior from 1940–1960. *Child Development*, 1964, **35**, 1021–1032.

Watson, J. S. Orientation-specific age changes in responsiveness to the face stimulus in young infants. Paper presented at the Convention of the American Psychological Association, Chicago, September, 1965.

Weikart, D. P., & Lambie, D. Z. Preschool intervention through a home teaching project. Paper presented at the Convention of the American Educational Research Association, 1968.

Weinberg, C. Family background and deviance or conformity to school expectations. *Journal of Marriage and the Family*, 1964, **26**, 89–91.

Weisberg, P. Social and nonsocial conditioning of infant vocalizations. *Child Development*, 1963, **34**, 377–388.

White, B. L. An experimental approach to the effects of experience on early human behavior. In J. P. Hill (Ed.), *Minnesota symposia on child psychology*, Volume 1. Minneapolis: University of Minnesota Press, 1966. Pp. 201–226.

Willerman, L., & Broman, S. H. Infant development, preschool IQ, and social class. *Child Development*, 1970, **41**, 69–77.

Williams, J. R., & Scott, R. B. Growth and development of Negro infants: IV. Motor development and its relationship to child-rearing practices in two groups of Negro infants. *Child Development*, 1953, **24**, 103–121.

Wimberger, H. C., & Kogan, K. L. Status behaviors in mother-child dyads in normal and clinic samples. *Psychological Reports*, 1972, **31**, 87–92.

Winterbottom, M. R. The relation of need for achievement to learning experiences in independence and mastery. In J. W. Atkinson (Ed.), *Motives in fantasy, action, and society*. Princeton, New Jersey: Van Nostrand, 1958. Pp. 453–478.

Wittenborn, J. R. A study of adoptive children. *Psychological Monographs*, 1956, **70**, 1–115.

Wittenborn, J. R. *The placement of adoptive children.* Springfield, Illinois: Thomas, 1957.

Wohlford, P., Santrock, J. W., Berger, S. E., & Liberman, D. Older brothers' influence on sex-typed, aggressive, and dependent behavior in father-absent children. *Developmental Psychology*, 1971, **4**, 124–134.

Wolff, P. H. Observations on the early development of smiling. In B. M. Foss (Ed.), *Determinants of infant behavior*. Volume 2. London: Methuen, 1963. Pp. 113–138.

Woods, M. B. The unsupervised child of the working mother. *Developmental Psychology*, 1972, **6**, 14–25.

Wortis, H., Bardach, J. L., Cutler, R., Rue, R., & Freedman, A. Child-rearing practices in a low socioeconomic group. *Pediatrics*, 1963, **32**, 298–307.

Wyler, R. S., Jr. Effect of child-rearing attitudes and behavior on children's responses to hypothetical social situations. *Journal of Personality and Social Psychology*, 1965, **2**, 480–486.

Yarrow, L. J. Maternal deprivation: toward an empirical, conceptual re-evaluation. *Psychological Bulletin*, 1961, **58**, 459–490.

Yarrow, L. J. Research in dimensions of early maternal care. *Merrill-Palmer Quarterly*, 1963, **9**, 101–114.

Yarrow, L. J., & Goodwin, M. S. Some conceptual issues in the study of mother–infant interaction. *American Journal of Orthopsychiatry*, 1965, **35**, 473–481.

Yarrow, M. R., Scott, P., DeLeeuw, L., & Heinig, C. Child-rearing in families of working and nonworking mothers. *Sociometry*, 1962, **25**, 122–140.

Yarrow, L. J., Rubenstein, J. L., & Pedersen, F. A. Dimensions of early stimulation. Differential effects on infant development. Papers presented at the meetings of the Society for Research in Child Development, Minneapolis, Minnesota, 1971.

Yarrow, M. R., Scott, P. M., & Waxler, C. Z. Learning concern for others. *Developmental Psychology*, 1973, **8,** 240–260.

Zelazo, P. Smiling to social stimuli: eliciting and conditioning effects. *Developmental Psychology*, 1971, **4,** 32–42.

Index

B
C 8
D 9
E 0
F 1
G 2
H 3
I 4
J 5